"Sam Bennett masterfully blenc... sonal in this easy-to-read, FUN-to-do approach. No matter what's up for you, you can find a way to begin and, if necessary, to begin again. These short chapters are so funny and warm. It's the perfect book for the stressed-out person — er...everyone."

— Linda Sivertsen, bestselling author of *Lives Charmed* and host of the *Beautiful Writers* podcast

Praise for Sam Bennett's *Get It Done*

"Like Steven Pressfield...Sam Bennett hears you, knows you, is you. She has been in your shoes, felt your fear, and been as stuck as you have. In an astonishing act of generosity, she's shared all that in this magnificent book."

— Seth Godin, author of *The Icarus Deception*

"Sam Bennett is refreshing in her positivity and achieves something rare — a how-to book that is funny and entertaining to read, and makes you feel good! Now, if you'll excuse me, I must go write an Oscar-winning screenplay. Or clean my room. One of the two — I'll figure it out."

— Rachel Dratch, actor, *Saturday Night Live* and *30 Rock*

"According to Sam Bennett, we don't need to be literally airborne in order to create: we can soar in only fifteen minutes a day. Her easy-to-do approach made me feel absolutely invincible....So have fun, don't ever let anyone tell you that you can't do it, and keep Sam around as your capable guide."

— from the foreword by Keegan-Michael Key, cocreator of *Key & Peele*, writer, actor, and producer

"Recommended for people who continually feel stymied in their pursuits."

— *Library Journal*

"If you need help getting things done (and who doesn't?) this book, written with love and passion, will help you."
— Ed O'Neill, actor, *Modern Family* and *Married with Children*

"Calling all artists! Are procrastination and perfectionism getting in the way of your sharing your creative gifts with the world? Through small, doable steps, *Get It Done* will help you make your big ideas real."
— Jennifer Lee, author of *The Right-Brain Business Plan*

"Sam Bennett is a genius — really.... *Get It Done* is the book you will come back to time and time again for inspiration, profound truths, humor, and one-of-a-kind practical tools."
— Amy Ahlers, author of *Big Fat Lies Women Tell Themselves*

"In these pages, artists and nonartists alike will find brilliant, tangible tools to tap into their inner organizing genius. Even when it feels impossible, we all can create bits of time, and Bennett's strategies put fifteen minutes a day to superb use."
— Marney K. Makridakis, author of *Creating Time*

"Fantastic for creative types of all stripes (actors, songwriters, visual artists, musicians, screenwriters), amateur, preprofessional, or professional. What Sam Bennett has to share is invaluable."
— Phil Swann, singer-songwriter, producer, author, and teacher

"Sam Bennett is the kind of insightful, articulate thinker who can make sense of the roadblocks we all face each day. Her book will help you get unstuck and on track, so that you can accomplish your goals." — Clate Mask, cofounder and CEO, Infusionsoft

"I've been meaning to read Sam Bennett's book for a while, but I haven't done it yet. I'm sure it is very good."
— Charlie Hartsock, executive producer, *Crazy Stupid Love* and *The Incredible Burt Wonderstone*

START
RIGHT
WHERE
YOU ARE

Also by Sam Bennett

365 Reasons to Write

By the Way, You Look Really Great Today: Selected Poems

*Get It Done: From Procrastination to Creative Genius
in 15 Minutes a Day*

*Less Crazy, More Money:
52 Secrets to Running a Serene, Profitable Business*

START RIGHT WHERE YOU ARE

How Little Changes Can Make a Big Difference for
Overwhelmed Procrastinators, Frustrated Overachievers,
and Recovering Perfectionists

SAM BENNETT

New World Library
Novato, California

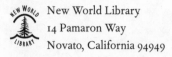

New World Library
14 Pamaron Way
Novato, California 94949

Text design by Tona Pearce Myers

Library of Congress Cataloging-in-Publication Data
Names: Bennett, Sam, [date]- author.
Title: Start right where you are : how little changes can make a big difference
    for overwhelmed procrastinators, frustrated overachievers, and recovering
    perfectionists / Sam Bennett.
Description: Novato, California : New World Library, [2016] | Includes index.
Identifiers: LCCN 2016031909 (print) | LCCN 2016046424 (ebook) | ISBN
    9781608684434 (pbk. : alk. paper) | ISBN 9781608684441 (Ebook)
Subjects: LCSH: Change (Psychology)
Classification: LCC BF637.C4 B45 2016 (print) | LCC BF637.C4 (ebook) | DDC
    158.1—dc23
LC record available at https://lccn.loc.gov/2016031909

First printing, November 2016
ISBN 978-1-60868-443-4
Ebook ISBN 978-1-60868-444-1
Printed in Canada on 100% postconsumer-waste recycled paper

New World Library is proud to be a Gold Certified Environmentally Responsible Publisher. Publisher certification awarded by Green Press Initiative. www.greenpressinitiative.org

10   9   8   7   6   5   4   3   2

For Luke
and a world of new beginnings

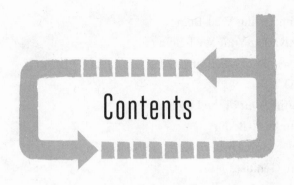

Contents

A Toast

I WANT TO RAISE A GLASS and say that I am so impressed with you right now.

I am impressed that you have committed your time, your intellect, and your emotional availability to this — this project of *you*. This project of you moving through your life in a way that feels better, calmer, kinder, more like the real you, less reactive, less self-sacrificing, more self-nourishing, and with more laughter.

Before we begin, I want you to see an email exchange I had with a potential client recently when he wrote to me about an online workshop I was offering:

> Hi Sam,
>
> While I applaud your efforts and wholeheartedly agree with your philosophy, the bottom line is that you are a motivational speaker and people feed off of your energy because that is something that they cannot provide for themselves. It's not about the book or the event, it's about your personality and charisma.... The problem is, once the book is read and the event attended we are usually back to square one.
>
> Anyway, I wish you success in your efforts and I will

continue to watch your webinars, you are really quite thera-
peutic but unless you are going to move in with me and give
me a kick in the pants 24/7, this stuff usually doesn't work.
   — B.

Here's what I wrote back:

Hi B.

I think that what you are saying is exactly true — but
only for about 80 percent of my audience.

That 80 percent attend a training or they read a book,
they get excited...and then they go right back to their same
old patterns and nothing changes.

As near as I can tell, that 80 percent number is true for
all personal development stuff, from gym memberships to
preachers to diet plans to financial strategies to everything
else on the planet. Shoot — most of us wear only 20 percent
of our wardrobe most of the time; the other 80 percent goes
unworn.

And I think that's fine.

If 80 percent of my audience are going to use me as a
source of temporary inspiration and entertainment, well,
then — what's wrong with that?

The remaining 20 percent, though...they actually do it.

They take the strategies and ideas I teach, and they run
with them, and they change.

They double their income.

They get out of destructive relationships.

They publish their book.

They get their "dream" business up and running.

My experience is that when people — well, I was going
to write "are ready to change," but I mean more than that —

when change becomes mandatory for them, they find the teacher who's right for them and they change.

So, B., if you suspect that you've reached the "mandatory" stage...or even if you'd just like a temporary shot of inspiration, I'd love to invite you to join us.

Thanks so much for taking the time to write.

Yours,

Sam

So here is my question for you:

Are you ready to be part of the 20 percent? Are you hungry to see real results? Because the techniques, mind-set shifts, and strategies I lay out here and at www.StartRightWhereYouAre.com have changed my life and the lives of thousands of my clients, and I know they can change yours, too.

Here's a toast to you and your wonderful self.

By the way, you look really great today.

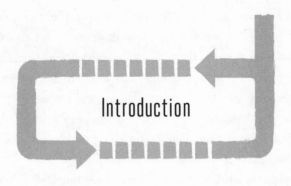

Introduction

I WAS TOTALLY MISERABLE. In the vise grip of depression, broke, exhausted, and completely fed up with myself. It was 1998, but it could have been any year of my adult life. Two of my friends — a couple — came over with a copy of a popular self-help book to cheer me up. I remember lying on the couch (I was too sad to even sit up straight) and seeing them, beaming at me. I kind of wanted to punch them.

After all, I was no stranger to self-help. I had been an actor all my life, first in my hometown of Chicago and then in Los Angeles, and I felt my career in the arts had already earned me a PhD in woo-woo. But I didn't have a better idea. So I thanked them, took the book, and started working with it.

I remember reading a part where the author described her day. She talked about waking up without an alarm, doing her prayer/meditation, having some tea, working with a client or two, lunch, a nap, some writing.... It sounded completely implausible to me. A nap? I couldn't even imagine — or, rather, I could just barely imagine — living like that.

My life was a chronically overscheduled mess of part-time jobs, gigs, classes, auditions, projects, and shows. I usually made just barely enough money, but not quite. I remember bursting

1

into tears in the middle of Target because I couldn't afford the sixteen bucks for a new pair of yoga pants (yoga pants being the official uniform of the artsy Angeleno). I was working hard all the time, and yet I kept feeling like I was falling further and further behind. I was desperately unhappy, and I was using "busy" as a narcotic. "Maybe," I thought, "if I'm busy enough, the only feeling I'll have is 'tired,' and I won't have to deal with the sneaking feeling that my life is an utter failure."

And guess what my life is like now? Let me put it this way — in the past eleven days I have:

- started writing a new book because I got a great idea in the middle of the night that will not leave me alone.
- bought a new car because it was time to retire my wonderful 2000 Honda Accord with 184,000 miles on it.
- spent two mind-melting-in-a-good-way days at a Byron Katie workshop in Ojai, California.
- screwed up my courage to introduce myself to Stephen Mitchell (Katie's husband), who is one of my literary heroes — I felt really shy, but I had to tell him how much his work has meant to me over the years, and I knew I couldn't keep encouraging you all to push past your perceived limitations if I wasn't willing to do the same.
- had a long, wonderful talk over an excellent bottle of wine with one of my oldest friends, who also happens to be a big TV star (and I got all the good Hollywood gossip).
- started a new paint-by-numbers picture, which is one of my favorite hobbies.
- paid a giant tax bill — which was great because it means business is good and getting better all the time, and plus I had salted the money away over the course of the year, so I could pay in full. My tax dude is very proud of me.
- taught seven classes — six online, one in person — to a

total of over 1,500 brilliant, creative people from all over the world.

- drove into LA to drop in on my favorite improv class, because I don't want to let my acting skills get rusty just because I moved to the beach, right?
- had two fun date nights with Luke, my sweetheart, plus our daily beach walks.
- made a lovely potato-leek soup from scratch from my battered old Julia Child cookbook — yum.
- attended a training webinar so I can stay up on all the latest email marketing technology.
- had a crown replaced (ugh), got my iPhone fixed (also ugh), had two short, effective team meetings with my fabulous crew, and finished reading two novels.

And I've got to say — it's not like this past eleven days is all that different from the rest of my calendar.

Now, before you decide that I might need to be punched, my life is not all sunshine and stardust — I work hard in and on my business, the Organized Artist Company, and I have just as many frustrations and heartbreaks as everyone else. But I don't have a boss. And I don't have a schedule, except for the one I create. And I get to spend all day doing work that I love, with people I love, in a place that I love. Life is sweet.

Over the past nineteen years, I must have written out Louise Hay's sentence "In the infinity of life where I am, all is perfect, whole, and complete," five grillion times. Finally, one day, I noticed I could really feel it was true. And now I know it's true with my whole heart. No matter what is happening, there is an infinity of life, and it is perfect, whole, and complete. My body and mind are perfect, whole, and complete. Even at the moment of my death (and I like to imagine *especially* at the moment of my death), all will be perfect, whole, and complete.

All of this is to say that this self-help stuff actually works. You, too, can be calmer, more creative, more loving, and more compassionate with yourself and others. You can feel more confident in yourself, and you can be more prosperous. You cannot escape the pain of life — no one can. Everyone gets the same amount of pain. (We'll talk more about that in chapter 33.) But you can increase your joy.

So that's what this book is for: to help you make the little changes that will lead to big joy. And big joy can make a big difference. It could even change the world.

Since the changes I suggest are so small, you might want to try each of them at least once, and then you can keep doing the ones you like and jettison the rest.

As a preview, here are a few of my favorite "little changes" that we'll be exploring in this book:

1. Get your cell phone out of the bedroom. Permanently. Give yourself back the gift of a morning stretch, a dozy cuddle, and the lovely liminal thoughts that come on waking. This is a good practice for everyone, and especially for those of you in the "frustrated overachiever" category.

2. Feel the Net. You are an inextricable and essential part of an Infinite Net of energy. You are one intersecting element in the larger picture of the whole universe. You are both much less significant and much more powerful than you may have been led to believe. If you fall into the "overwhelmed procrastinator" category, and you often catch yourself thinking that there's "not enough time," you might find this image of the Infinite Net quite calming.

3. Schedule some Happy Grown-Up Naked Time. Whether you are in a relationship or not, start making time to just be nude and play. Spending a goal-free half-hour rediscovering what makes you giggle, tingle, and thrill is a terrific way to reconnect with the wisdom of your body and also have a little fun. If you have ever applied your "perfectionist" self to your body image or sexuality, you might find this practice particularly freeing.

4. Acknowledge that feeling overwhelmed is a choice. Overwhelmed is an overused word that can mean a lot of different things. We'll work on identifying the actual source of your overwhelm in chapters 8, 11, and 16, and take specific steps to mitigate it. Nothing good ever came from the curious inaction caused by the mental chaos known as *overwhelm*. You might want to read the previous sentence aloud: see if you can feel the truth of it for yourself.

5. Turn your complaints into requests. Quit complaining. Permanently. If you have a request, make it. If you have a suggestion, offer it. If you want things to change, then be the instrument of change. Approach the troubling elements of your world with a gentle and courageous spirit. If you want to change your life, you're going to have to start taking 100 percent responsibility for it, and complaining is the hobbyhorse of a victim mentality. You're better than that. Part of the *recovering* in *recovering perfectionist* has to do with finding new, more productive ways to channel your discernment, your good judgment, and your meticulous attention to detail.

> Nothing good ever came from the curious inaction caused by mental chaos known as overwhelm.

6. Release that which no longer serves you. Clutter is the residue of old decisions, and it just plain takes up too much room. Free yourself from your old stuff so you have space to become your new self. We'll even clear the mental clutter from your "Dream Closet" in chapter 49. You'll be amazed at how much more energy you have when you — and your stuff — have some breathing room.

7. Stop having imaginary arguments with other people. It's so tempting to replay key moments from your life in your mind, usually with the dialogue rewritten. Or to imagine future events in which you not only look fabulous but manage to say the perfect thing, every time. Your "overachieving" self flaunts the vision of this more perfect version of self at you and makes you believe that you should be better, smarter, quicker than you are (or were). Start using your imagination in more self-supporting ways.

8. Make some 5-Minute Art about it. Creativity — it's not just for artists anymore. This 5-Minute Art concept is one of the most flat-out useful ideas in this book, so let's talk about it now.

Here's the plan: The next time you feel upset, sad, frustrated, furious, or trapped by the past, take five minutes and make some art about how you are feeling. Draw a picture, write a poem, do a little dance, sing a little song. This art does not have to be good. In fact, I think it's better if you make it deliberately bad, and you have permission to throw it away as soon as you're done. Why am I suggesting that you make some bad, disposable art? Because feelings just want to be felt.

Once a feeling knows that it's been felt, the energy of it is released and can transform into a different feeling. You've had that experience — when a good cry is followed by a feeling of deep peace, or when an angry outburst transmogrifies into a fit of the giggles. On the other hand, when you keep your feelings locked away, they often grow stronger, darker, and more powerful. Worse yet, whatever steps you take to avoid your feelings will end up sabotaging you. So making some 5-Minute Art is a quick, easy, and even delightful way to activate the pressure-release valve.

> Feelings just want to be felt.

Externalizing your feelings also gives you a new perspective on them. Using color, rhythm, images, and melody to give form to your emotions allows you to understand them in a new way. And it can allow others to better understand you as well.

My indispensable team leader at the Organized Artist Company, Leonore Tjia, once found herself feeling completely swamped with demands from our students and fearful that she was about to let everyone down. The anxiety was paralyzing her. Luckily, she had the presence of mind to go to the whiteboard in her office and sketch an image that captured how she was feeling. She texted me a photo of it, with the caption, "This drawing is of me as a sad border collie, weeping by the pond because she let all the little lambs drown." This little cartoon was so sweet and so melancholic that she started to laugh at herself. In the freedom of laughter, she found renewed energy, and a reminder that what she had been experiencing as stress was really just her desire to do a good job run amok. You can see Leonore's drawing at www.StartRightWhereYouAre.com.

During one of my three-day events, Marie, a tall woman with a slightly librarian-ish demeanor, raised her hand and politely said, "Sam, I hear you say, 'Make some art about it' all the time, and I'm still not sure what you mean. Could you give an example?"

"Sure," I said. "If you were to make up a little song right now about how it feels to not understand, how would it go?"

She started moving her head from side to side in a funny tick-tock motion and chanted, "I don't get it, I don't get it, I don't get it, I don't get it," and the whole room burst into laughter. She laughed too, and said, "Okay! *Now* I get it!" The action of turning her frustration into a little ditty cheered her right up. It also allowed all of us to recognize, sympathize with, and participate in her feelings. I still sing Marie's little song to myself whenever I feel like I'm being obtuse, and it takes the feeling of being dense and airless and it opens up all the windows and lets the cool breeze blow right through.

Your reaction to your 5-Minute Art may not be humorous, of course. You may discover that you are much sadder, much calmer, or much more furious than you thought. One student sent me a copy of a dark drawing she had made of a big, black bird that covered almost the whole page. She said she hadn't realized how unhappy she was until she saw her own drawing. Recognition is the first step toward transformation.

If you're thinking to yourself, "But, Sam, I'm not artistic," remember that once you were a child who cheerfully drew pictures, sang songs, danced, and played with clay. You were completely unconcerned about how "good" your work was, and you simply reveled in the playful expression of your spirit. Tap into that still-existing childlike part of yourself, and you'll be amazed at how easily the 5-Minute Art will flow right out of you.

> Recognition is the first step toward transformation.

In the rest of this book, we'll talk about how you can:

- amp up your intuition and inner knowing
- get over your fear of success
- figure out how to pick a project that's going to be really great for you
- find a tribe or community of like-minded people who will support you, celebrate you, and cherish your involvement in their lives

All the things you keep telling yourself you want to do, be, or have are possible for you, if you are willing to take it one step at a time. No matter how long you've been dreaming your dreams, they are still alive, still possible. Just because they haven't happened up to now doesn't mean they won't happen. And just because your life, career, or projects haven't gone the way you may have wanted doesn't mean they are not going well. No matter what has happened to you up to now, you have an opportunity to create a new story, beginning right now.

Take a deep breath.
Notice the good in this moment.
Because this is all you have.
Start now.
Start right where you are.

1. ⟶ How to Create a Miracle

You know the times when you have had a goal or a dream, worked hard to make it happen, and then...just...nothing? No movement. Can't get traction. So frustrating, right?

Other times, you have a goal or a dream, and you take just very few baby steps toward it, and suddenly it feels as if the universe itself comes rushing in to support you. It seems that all you have to do is put out a little energy, and you get a big tidal wave of energy back. Maybe you have an idea in your head about moving house, and the next thing you know, the perfect place becomes available, and it's easily affordable, and you get to just swan right in. Or maybe you're dreaming of meeting the perfect business partner, and then, out of the blue, that person is standing right in front of you, ready and willing. It's wonderful when that happens, isn't it?

Ask around and you'll hear a lot of different explanations for why sometimes you get what you want, and sometimes you don't. People may invoke the power of a strong intention, vibration, divine timing, angels, destiny, manifestation skills, karma, luck, or happenstance. But I have a different theory — and please note that I mean *theory* in the sense of an interesting way to think about things, not in the scientific sense.

Imagine that you are standing in the exact center of your world: that you are the sun, the hub, the eye of the storm. Now imagine that there are lines, like spokes on a wheel, or like the individual puffs on a dandelion, extending out from you that connect you with everything else. Those lines represent your relationship with the potentiality of all things. Every opportunity, every relationship, every everything can be connected to you through those spokes. Can you see it?

Now, if you take one small step in any direction, can you imagine how those lines shift in their relationship with you? Now each line is at a slightly different angle. And so maybe there are some spokes that weren't reaching you before that now prod you square in the chest. Or maybe the angle of one spoke has become more oblique, so that there is no longer a direct path between that thing and you. Other spokes that were right in your center are now maybe a bit off to the side.

This is why a tiny shift can cause a big difference. Can you imagine that for yourself? Right now, think of something that you want that has eluded you. Maybe it's a new relationship, or a baby, or a creative project. Can you imagine yourself shifting just a few degrees and intersecting your energy with the potentiality of that thing? Can you imagine how easily even the unlikeliest goal might be achieved? I hear stories every day from my students and clients in which they've finally decided to write their book, and the next thing they know, they find themselves deep in conversation with a friendly stranger who turns out to be a literary agent. Or just when they decide they're ready to start dating, the phone rings, and Mr. or Ms. Perfect Fabulous Person is on the line.

I've heard the analogy of a rocket ship to describe this, too: if the trajectory of a rocket ship to the sun is off by just one degree, its course is dramatically altered. In fact, it will end up over 1.6 million miles from its original destination. Could it be that you are just one degree away from everything you've ever wanted?

When you move, your perspective — the angle at which you see things — shifts. Experiment for yourself: from the position you are in right now, turn your head like an owl, and notice what you can see. For example, I'm at my desk, and if I turn my head as far as I can to the right and use as much of my peripheral vision as possible, I can see a pair of shoes on the floor (I really ought

> Could it be that you are just one degree away from everything you've ever wanted?

to be better about putting my shoes away) and the corner of the wooden Swedish trunk that my father handed down to me. If I turn my head all the way to the left, I can see part of my bookshelf and some of the big green chair that sits in front of the bookshelf.

Do this right now and note what you can see.

Now move your body a bit in any direction. Look around again, peering as far as you can to your right and left. You'll notice that your view has changed a bit. I can now see more of the trunk and also past it, to the coffee table. Craning around to my left, I can now see all of the green chair.

So my theory in action looks like this: when you decide that you want something and you move toward it physically, emotionally, or spiritually, then your movement opens up new pathways by which things can appear in your life. Even a very small step (physical, emotional, or spiritual) can cause a radical change in your relationship to the thing you want. Even a small shift in perspective can allow you to see new opportunities.

And those times when you wished and hoped for things to change, but nothing happened? It's because you never actually moved. You stayed put. So your relationship to the potentiality of all things remained the same, and you kept getting the same results, over and over and over and over again.

So we get to cocreate our reality with the potentiality of all things through our decisions and our actions. And we get to see the deep truth in the axiom, "If you always do what you've always done, you'll always get what you've always gotten."

With a one-degree shift in your internal navigation, suddenly you can do things like:

- complete the projects that are dear to your heart
- change your relationship with your body and improve your physical health
- double your income (this is not a far-fetched marketing claim: I have actually done this several times, and so have several of my clients)
- transform your relationships with people who are important to you
- get your work out in the world
- transcend your visibility issues
- overcome a bad past or old stories

Change doesn't have to take hours of arduous work, and you don't have to wait to start. Think of it this way: you cannot lose thirty pounds all at once right now. But you can start behaving like someone who is thirty pounds thinner right now. You can eat what that thinner person eats and you can treat yourself the way you would if you had already met that goal. Similarly, you cannot build a successful business right now, but you can start behaving like a successful businessperson and start taking the daily steps to get there. Step by step you can go leaps and bounds.

Those little shifts will feel radical. Even those one-degree shifts will feel like the world is tilting off its axis, because for you, it is. But if you can keep your sea legs — if you can hang on through the temporary discomfort of change — you will see results.

> Step by step you can go leaps and bounds.

Maybe you will develop the ability to look in the mirror and notice what looks beautiful about you instead of automatically reciting the litany of things you think are wrong with you. Maybe you'll find you can enjoy a conversation with somebody that you haven't talked to in a long time. Maybe you will find it easier to be more intimate, to be more open, to be more present. I don't know how this is going to unfold for you. But I guarantee you that if you do the work, if you're willing to endure the super-uncomfortable feeling that your world is changing, you'll see some wonderful changes in your life.

LITTLE CHANGES ACTION STEP: If you were going to allow yourself to make a one-degree shift today, what would that be? Would you choose to be 1 percent more courageous? More joyful? More outspoken? More kind? Pick a word that you would like to be able to say describes you, and now — right now — find a way to be 1 percent more that way.

2. → The You in the Center of You

YOU USUALLY HEAR THE TERM *self-centered* meant as a criticism. But, thanks to the hub-and-spokes image, whenever I hear it, I think, "Yes. I am in the center of myself. My self is my center."

When you are centered in yourself, you are the still center around which the wheel of your life spins. The circumstances of your life are the outer rim of the wheel. You want to stay in the middle, but it's all too easy to let yourself get pulled out on the edge of the wheel so that as events happen, you end up spinning along with them. You get tumbled.

Learning how to stay in the center of yourself means developing some discipline so that you aren't pulled off-center by other people's opinions, bad news, or success. When you really get practiced at staying right in the center of you, things may spin around you, but you do not spin, you stay grounded and true to yourself.

You don't have to let your circumstances determine your happiness anymore. You can stay in the center of your self and be able to feel the joy of your life no matter what is happening on the outside.

So let's put you in the center of your life.

I recommend that you access the free audio version of this short meditation at www.StartRightWhereYouAre.com, because I think you'll find it easier to visualize the concepts if you listen to me say it rather than reading it silently. You could also make a recording of yourself reading it and play it back with your eyes closed.

And if you're the kind of person who avoids meditation, no worries — I invite you to try only the simple, effective breathing pattern. I have been doing this breathing pattern for over twenty years, and it has helped me through panic attacks, boring sermons, bumpy airplane rides, Los Angeles traffic, audition jitters, and insomnia. It's a miracle worker.

Here's the pattern:

Inhale for a count of four, hold for a count of seven, exhale for a count of eight.

That's it. 4:7:8.

You can just do it once and get a nice effect, although I usually like to do it three times. You can also keep going and repeat the cycle as many times as you like. Once, at a party, I stayed up until 5 AM, sitting on the couch, counting out this breathing pattern with a friend who was having a bad experience on some psychotropic drugs. She said later that the breathing kept her from "completely freaking the freak out." So, while I'm not making any medical claims here, it's good for defreaking.

I like this breathing cycle because it is so simple, and because the counting pattern is just unusual enough to distract me from my thinking. It returns me to my center.

Here's the text of the meditation to read, read aloud, or download as audio:

> If you're somewhere where you can close your eyes, go ahead and close your eyes. If you can't or don't want to close your eyes, just soften your gaze a little bit. Let things go just a little blurry. Soften your gaze, soften your heart. And now feel the very center of you. Feel the energy in the

center of yourself like it's the core of something, like the heart of a tree — the heartwood. Focus on that energy in the center of you. And let that center beam be really clear and strong. And let everything else relax around it. So your hands can relax. Your feet can relax. Your belly can relax. The back of your neck, your jaw, your tongue, your heart, your joints, your mind, your judgment. Feel that beaming energy drop down into the earth so you are connected to the living planet. And feel it extend upward out the top of your head so you are connected to the sky above.

Now imagine that the beam is illuminated. Imagine that it glows. See if you can turn an imaginary rheostat to make it glow more brightly. Experiment with the color, intensity, and size of your illuminated center beam.

And just staying in the center of yourself, we're going to inhale, two, three, four; hold, two, three, four, five, six, seven; exhale, two, three, four, five, six, seven, eight. Inhale, two, three, four; hold, two, three, four, five, six, seven; exhale, two, three, four, five, six, seven, eight. Inhale, two, three, four; hold, two, three, four, five, six, seven; exhale, two, three, four, five, six, seven, eight.

Thank you. Thank you for doing that with me.

There are several versions of this meditation, designed to support you as you move through the material in this book. Feel free to use them however you want — there's no need to be all precious about it and feel like you have to light candles or do it perfectly or anything. Just play around with the ideas, do the work that interests you, and leave the rest for some other time. Do what feels easy. Little changes, remember?

LITTLE CHANGES ACTION STEP: Right now, do the 4:7:8 breathing three times. Repeat at will.

3. ⟶ Buckle Up, Because I'm About to Get Deep Here, People

I CREATED the Start Right Where You Are workshop and this book so that you and I could talk more about the inner game of leading a creatively and spiritually fulfilling life.

I love offering material that is both functional and doable. My first book was called *Get It Done: From Procrastination to Creative Genius in 15 Minutes a Day*, for Pete's sake. I'm a practical person, and I really enjoy teaching about creative productivity.

But eventually I realized that I was leaving out a big, important chunk of information about being centered in yourself and connected to everything, which is what had enabled me to go from being broke and exhausted all the time to not-broke and not-exhausted all the time. It was time for me to start talking about the inner journey.

If you don't believe that you can be creatively fulfilled, well, it doesn't really matter what productivity tools I give you, does it? And if you're not sure that it's really okay for you to be calm and successful and loved no matter what, then no amount of helpful advice will change your patterns. So we need to start at the very beginning — at the very center of you — and work outward. We start with your soul.

This means that I will, in fact, be talking about God. And it's not important to me whether or not you believe in God, or what you call God. I trust that you're a sophisticated enough person that you can make whatever mental substitutions you need to make. I want to be clear: I'm not proselytizing. I don't want to turn anyone off or freak anybody out. I know some of you have been really burned by the whole God thing, and I truly don't care if you're religious or spiritual or philosophical or none of the above. I'm not trying to position myself as any kind of spiritual leader or teacher. I'm just using the words *God* or *the Net* to signify that eternal thing that is bigger than us.

My partner, Luke, is a committed atheist. He's done quite a bit of reading about the topic of God, and he tells me that what I mean when I talk about God is not what most people mean when they talk about God. So I'll get into a little bit more of my definition of God later on, but for now, I want you to identify for yourself what word you like to use to describe the mystery of life.

You've felt that sense of mystery when you gaze at a sunset or at the mountains. Maybe you've felt it when you spend time with animals, or when you have been in the "flow," physically or creatively. So you can call it *Love* or *the Divine* or *Spirit* or *Source* or *Buttons the Clown* if you want. I'm going to use *God* or *the Net*, because those words work for me, plus it's less awkward than having to say, "that eternal, mysterious thing that is bigger than us" every time. (And really, if you want to go through this book and cross out the word *God* and replace it with an *X* or another word, I think that's great. Do what works for you.)

Let me walk you through a two-minute exercise so you can experience what I mean by *the Net*, rather than discuss it further. Experience is much more important than theory.

You can find the free downloadable audio for this exercise at www.StartRightWhereYouAre.com.

Start by shifting around in your seat a little bit. Just wiggle slightly or get up and turn around — something to signal to your body that we're up to something different. And let's go back to that image of your heartwood, the center of you, the core of you. Just feel that energy in the middle of you and feel it drop down into the earth and extend upward toward the sky.

Focus in on this heartwood core of you that's now plugged into the living earth, that's connected to the sky and the stars and the sun. Imagine that that beam glows — that it has a color, and an intensity. And visualize all the spokes radiating out from you like a dandelion puff, extending out, out, out, into infinity. The spokes glow, too.

And now imagine all the other people who are reading or praying or meditating right now. Imagine their center, and the glowing spokes emanating from them.

And now imagine everyone else — all the other people walking around, grocery shopping, napping, working — and see that they all have a lit-up center and spokes, too. Can you see how everyone's spokes are crisscrossing? Together, we make a giant Net of energy. Imagine this giant Net. Can you see it in your mind? Can you see how your energy intersects with that person's or that person's or that person's, all the way on the other side of the globe and off into unseen worlds? Can you feel it? There is energy constantly moving through this Net.

And now, imagine that all the other living things are also lit up and have spokes and are connected energetically with each other. All the animals, all the trees, the sea creatures, the plants, even the minerals in the earth are suffused with energy and are part of this Net.

Play around with the image of the Net a little bit. Can you feel how "it is the ocean and you are the wave"? Can you lean back into the Net and feel supported by it — by all of life? See if you can pull on the Net a little bit. Give it a tug and pull some of the energy of the Net into you. Do you feel it? Feel the energy of the Net come into your body. Feel your connectedness to all things.

Can you imagine that as you connect with the Net, your inner radiance gets dialed up?

I love to imagine you, all lit up from within, connected to all the other lit-up elements of the Net. Some things you are connected to directly, and others may seem far away, but we are all part of one perfect whole.

Notice that no matter how brightly you shine, you don't take anything away from the Net. The Net of energy is in constant motion, and it is all equally yours and not yours. This is how we know that nothing ever goes away, and nothing is ever wasted — because it is all part of the Net. The Net is an imagining of the first law of thermodynamics: energy can be converted from one form into another, but it cannot be created or destroyed. In other words, you can't break the Net. You can't destroy it. You can't push it too hard. It is much, much bigger than you are. And still you are an essential part of it.

We are just one expression of this energy on this planet. The energy of the Net is eternal; it is the alpha and the omega. We are an expression of the Divine. We are cocreating reality with the Net. We are the hands and feet of God.

If you like, you may close the meditation now by breathing 4:7:8 a few times and bring yourself back to current time and space. Please keep the image of the Net in your mind, though, because we have more to explore.

You cannot be separate from this Net. You cannot be separate from this web of energy. The entire Net is your legacy: the gift that has been handed to you and that you, in turn, pass on. In other words, you cannot be separate from God. You may sometimes feel like you are, but that's you doing that to you. And it's as false as believing that the sun disappears when it's raining. The sun is still there, above the clouds. The Net knows that you are never not a part of it.

Part of your work is to stop arguing with that divine energy that is trying to express itself through you. Stop believing that maybe it's not right, or it's not yours, or you're too much this or you're not enough that. You are everything. You are, literally, made of stardust. As Neil deGrasse Tyson said in the first episode of *The Universe*, "Recognize that the very molecules that make up your body, the atoms that construct the molecules, are traceable to the crucibles that were once the centers of high-mass stars.... We are all connected. To each other, biologically, to the earth, chemically, and to the rest of the universe, atomically.... We are in the universe, and the universe is in us."*

Accept the energy. Plug into the energy of the cosmos. Let it heal you. Let it come through you to heal others. Let God express God's self through you exactly as you are right now. This begins right now. And this has been happening the whole time. You're just tapping into it with a bit more consciousness and deliberation.

You can see in your mind's eye how the activity of this Net can defy logic, expectation, and conventional wisdom. If everything is interconnected, no wonder quantum leaps are possible. No wonder people and events can arrive in our lives suddenly and unannounced. And no wonder once-in-a-lifetime opportunities come around every single day.

In my heart of hearts, what I really believe about God, what I believe God is, is that Net. I don't perceive God as a moral force. I don't believe that the Net cares, really, what we do, any more than nature cares what we do. There are laws of cause and effect, certainly, and those pertain to both nature and the Net. We, the people, care. We, the people in your community, would rather that you not covet our neighbor's wife or cheat or steal or dishonor your parents. But as far as the Net is concerned, you are fine. You

---

* *The Universe*, produced by Matt Hickey, History Channel, 2007.

are forgiven. You are valuable. You are essential. You are loved, and you are love.

I imagine the Net makes a sound that I call the Benevolent Hum. It's the song the universe sings. It might sound like *Om*. And this humming energy, this creation, is moving — breath moving, cells dividing, things coming into form and leaving form, water to steam to clouds to rain to water. Being born and dying. It's an infinite cycle. And we are fortunate enough to be present in this form in this moment. What a blessing.

God is the Benevolent Hum.

So when I say *God*, or *the Net*, that's what I mean.

LITTLE CHANGES ACTION STEP: Right now, make some 5-Minute Art expressing one moment from your life when you felt connected to the Net, to that which is bigger than you, to the beauty, grace, and mystery of life. (Need a suggestion? Write two short paragraphs about a powerful encounter you've had with nature, describing both what you experienced and what it meant to you.)

4. ➡ Rested, Fed, Meditated, Walked, Cuddled, and Creatively Satisfied

IF YOU'RE GOING TO STAY CONNECTED to the Net and to the center of yourself, you're going to have to start taking better care of yourself.

Taking care of yourself isn't selfish. In fact, it's the opposite of selfish. When you spend all your time giving to others and you're tired, stressed out, overwhelmed, and exhausted, you are no fun to be around. In fact, making the rest of us deal with you when you are a humorless wreck is really quite selfish of you. (I'm kidding. We love you.)

On the other hand, when you are rested, fed, meditated, walked, cuddled, and creatively satisfied, you bring your best self to the world. You have more to give, and you give more freely. You think more clearly, and you don't sweat the small stuff.

Here are some behaviors that my existing and former clients have demonstrated that, to me, indicated an imbalance in the whole "taking care of you" thing:

1. Sharon refused to go to the doctor, even though she'd been feeling lousy for a while. (It turned out she had severe anemia, which is easily treated but can be life-threatening if ignored.)

> When you are rested, fed, meditated, walked, cuddled, and creatively satisfied, you bring your best self to the world.

2. Diana always works through lunch. Doesn't everybody? (Nope.)
3. Jason couldn't help saying yes every time someone asked a favor of him. He had always just assumed that owning a truck meant that he was automatically obligated to help people move.
4. Nancy tolerated long, energy-draining phone calls from "friends" who just wanted to complain.
5. Risa made long, energy-draining calls to her friends just to complain.
6. Claire would buy new clothes for the kids but not for herself.
7. Belinda would go shopping to buy new clothes and end up just buying the exact same thing she always wore. (That's not shopping, that's replacing.)
8. Kelly wore old, worn-out shoes. (Nobody notices the scuff-marked heels, do they? Um, yes. We do.)
9. Ava kept the Mother's Day gift of expensive scented lotion in the cabinet, feeling it was too good for every day. When she finally felt like she had an occasion special enough, she found that it had spoiled.
10. When other people asked Ethan, who was caring for two young kids and his ailing mother, if they could help him out, he would automatically say, "Oh, no thanks," even though he really could have used an extra hand. He didn't want to appear needy, even in his time of need.
11. Daniel refused to get new clothes because he was going to lose weight any day now.
12. Ashley thought it would be a waste of money to hire a great coach (or therapist or trainer or teacher) to help her achieve her goals. She kept thinking she should be able to do it all by herself, but so far, anyway, her actions haven't matched her ambition.

13. Christopher was not keeping his professional skills or his résumé up to date. (Even just keeping a hard copy of your résumé around so you can make little notes on it whenever you get promoted, finish a big project, or obtain a new degree or certification will make it easier to get a new job when you want one, or to negotiate for a better salary in the job you have.)

14. Megan, an artist, didn't spend enough time cultivating professional relationships, so her circle was small and her resources were limited.

15. Hannah never upgraded her computer. Nor did she back up. (A disaster waiting to happen.)

16. Victoria never allowed herself to sleep in, even when she could.

17. Kayla would fall asleep in movies because she was so exhausted.

18. Kevin had clutter. A lot of clutter. (We'll talk about the clutter thing more in chapter 47.)

You might feel like it is impossible to find enough time in the day to be well rested, intellectually stimulated, physically active, and well put together, but I assure you that it's entirely possible. In fact, you probably know someone like that — someone who always looks great, is rarely tardy, and always seems to have a good attitude. That person is that way because of his or her habits. And I promise you, it takes exactly the same amount of time to *not* take care of yourself as it does to take care of yourself.

> It takes exactly the same amount of time to *not* take care of yourself as it does to take care of yourself.

How do I know? Because everyone gets the same twenty-four hours a day. No one gets more. Some people take that twenty-four hours and manage to raise kids, write books, have hot sex, forgive themselves their belly pooch, and all the other stuff you keep thinking you'll get to "someday — when it's not so crazy." Guess what, honey? The crazy is not your circumstances. The crazy is you.

When you start treating yourself well, you will find that everything else gets a lot easier:

- When you are rested, your mind is clear, and you make better decisions.
- When you are well fed, you are less reactive, and you can more swiftly process information.
- When you are stretching yourself creatively, you become a better problem solver.
- When you feel great about yourself and how you look, your confidence empowers you.

You would never let a child run around ragged, exhausted, underfed, and undercuddled, would you? So please, stop thinking that you taking excellent care of yourself is a luxury you can't afford. Because the opposite is true: neglecting yourself is a luxury you can't afford.

The world needs you. The world needs your good work. The world needs your love, your compassion, your insight, and your great good humor. Especially when things get tense, like in traffic jams and at the airport and in line at the grocery store behind the person who's trying to use an expired coupon and at family events (bless!) and at that horrible monthly sales meeting — and everywhere else you are, too.

> The world needs your good work.

LITTLE CHANGES ACTION STEP: Stop rushing. Give yourself a moment of transition between activities. Before you get out of the car, or go into the meeting, or pick up the phone, take three deep breaths (4:7:8) and think something nice about yourself. Just a microsecond "reset" will allow you to be more present and attentive, even when your schedule is jam-packed.

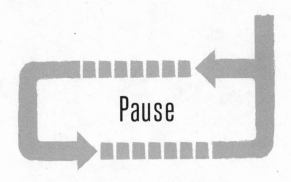

Pause

Daily Grind

Dear God,

The daily grind has got my Spirit by the neck.

There are too many things to do, and I am exhausted down to My bones.

Even the things I like to do feel like a chore, and in all this ordinary chaos,

There is no room for me to make art.

But I hear you whisper that I was not created in your image To run errands.

And that a year from now, no one will remember the imperfect nutritional value of tonight's dinner, but everyone will remember the piece I create.

So, just for today, I will claim some time — ironclad, nonnegotiable, uncompromising, turn-off-the-phone time — to do the work that you designed me to do.

That is my promise to you, so that I might fulfill your promise of me.

Love,
Me

5. ➡ Nothing Is More Important Than Your Well-Being

I'M GOING TO INTRODUCE YOU to a wonderful and somewhat radical phrase, and I want you to write it down right now: "Nothing is more important than my well-being."

You picked up this book because you want your life to be better. And I am here to tell you that the only way your life is going to get better is if you start treating yourself better. So say this phrase aloud and see how you feel about it: "Nothing is more important than my well-being."

As we move through this work, you're going to need to repeat this phrase to yourself over and over again. We're not just putting self-care on the list as an afterthought. We are moving it right up to the very top of the list. In fact, it might become the whole list.

I realize how crazy that might sound. After all, I once walked around with pneumonia for six weeks because I was so busy holding down three part-time jobs (delivering flowers, which was miserable; office receptionist, which was unspeakably dull; and teaching acting, which was great), producing a play at my theater company, appearing in a successful late-night improv comedy show, and still keeping up with the housework that I didn't notice that my bad cold had turned into something much more serious. The idea of taking time for my own self-care was so remote that I became quite, quite ill.

What thoughts start racing through your mind when you imagine letting the betterment of your own well-being make your decisions for you? "That would be so selfish.... I would never do anything for anyone else.... Too many other people rely on me." But is that really true? I bet that when you are well cared for and your inner monologue is friendly, you actually get more done for the people around you. And what if everyone took great care of themselves? What if everyone was well fed and well rested and had a kindly inner monologue going on? Could be a whole new world.

Let's unpack this "Nothing is more important than your well-being" a bit more.

The negative voices in your head are not more important than your well-being. Your old stories are not more important than your well-being. Even the demands of your family, the pressures of your job, and the good opinion of others are not more important than your well-being. I'm not saying those things are not at all important, of course. They are important. But they are not more important.

Let's keep going: Your bank account, or what you believe to be the reality of your finances, is not more important than your well-being. Your ego and your big idea about who you are or who you're supposed to be or where you should be by now are not more important than your well-being. Your desire to be right is not more important than your well-being. Your desire to be liked, your desire to be appreciated, your desire to be approved of are not more important than your well-being.

Pause right there: Can you imagine if you put your well-being ahead of your desire to be approved of? Sit with that for a second. What does that look like? Let's say you've got a morning meditation walk scheduled, and suddenly you get a call telling you that a client is freaking out. Your self-doubt might take over, and you might sacrifice the walk so that you don't feel like a bad businessperson or just a plain old bad person. But if your well-being is the most important thing, then you go on your walk with the understanding that you will return shortly, better able to be of service to your client. Can you see how radical this is?

Make some notes for yourself about what challenges might show up and appear to be more important than your well-being. (The kids, the boss calling, a headache, a phone call, social media, fatigue, an old story that makes you ask, "Why even bother?")

What are some of the things that you currently believe are more important than your well-being? Go ahead and write them down. You need to identify these things and put big pink name tags on them so that you recognize them when they show up later. Because, believe me, they will absolutely show up later.

I once had a client named Maryann who wanted to start a coaching business while still working full time. When I challenged her to spend the weekend calling potential clients, she said, "Oh, I would, but I'm scheduled to work on a Habitat for Humanity house this weekend. It's a work thing — my office does this every year."

"Nope. You're just going to have to cancel," I replied. Maryann actually gasped. I continued, "Tell them you're sorry, but someone else will have to take your place. Anyone can help build that house, but only you can build your business."

Now, I adore volunteering, and I certainly understand the value of officemates gathering to do community work. I think it's wonderful, and I'd like to see more of that kind of behavior. But I could tell that if Maryann was willing to put that commitment ahead of her dreams, then she would put everything ahead of her dreams, which meant that her business would stay just a dream. So, even though she felt like she was going to get demerits on her Good Girl card, she withdrew from the event and found a replacement. Later on she told me that not only did the weekend of calls have a good effect on her new business, but the officemate who replaced her deeply enjoyed the opportunity and began volunteering more regularly. So in fact, Maryann's willingness to be "selfish" ended up being a triple blessing.

LITTLE CHANGES ACTION STEP: Write down five examples of how exchanging some of your self-sacrificing behaviors for more self-nourishing behaviors could benefit everyone involved. For example, perhaps delegating a recurring errand to the teenage driver in your house could both be a gesture of respect and additional responsibility earned to your teen and give you a much-needed break. This might bring better balance to the whole family. Or maybe there's a volunteer gig that's become more draining than satisfying, and so stepping back from that commitment might give someone else a chance to be a leader in that community. Making a change might give you more time for art and fun as well as giving the organization a chance to deepen their bench of volunteers they can count on.

6. ➡ Six Ways to Take Control of Your Time

TIME IS SO SLIPPERY, isn't it? The time spent in line at the bank goes so slowly you can practically feel yourself wrinkling up as you stand there. But the hour you spend on the phone with your best friend whizzes by. And remember the moment when they first put the baby in your arms? Time ceased to exist entirely.

I hear from... well, from almost everyone, really, that they have trouble managing their time, so here are a few critical little changes you can make today that will help you stop struggling with the idea that there's never enough time and start enjoying the time you have.

Get Your Cell Phone out of the Bedroom

The first few moments on waking are an important time of day, especially for the creative, sensitive, and overworked person.

Your reticular activating system is the part of your brain that helps regulate your levels of consciousness and tells you when to wake up. (If you've ever wondered how one tiny sound, like the creak of a floorboard, can wake you out of a deep sleep, you can thank your reticular activating system. Isn't the body amazing?) Science tells us that your waking-up time is one of your most creative moments in the day, because your brain has spent the night organizing your memories and thoughts, and your body is relaxed, so you are more likely to make unusual connections between ideas, discover new solutions to problems, and have especially entertaining thoughts first thing.

Nothing ruins the cozy mood of a morning like a cell phone.

There is nothing on the internet that cannot wait for twenty minutes while you do some mindful breathing and think grateful thoughts.

There is a pure, animal pleasure in allowing yourself to gradually come to wakefulness, to stretch, to doze, to cuddle, and to greet the day with a big, delicious yawn. Even just thirty seconds of 4:7:8 breathing before you leap into action can benefit your whole day.

"But I use my phone for an alarm clock," I hear you protest. Right. Cut that out. Go get an alarm clock. "But I have teenagers — what if they call in the middle of the night?" Okay, then put a little shelf or charging station near the door to your bedroom and leave your phone there. You don't have to be out of touch if there's an emergency. You just don't want to begin each morning as though it *is* an emergency.

Don't Check Email or Social Media as a Way of Easing into Your Workday

You've got your mug of coffee or tea, and you're settling in at your desk. "Okay," you think, "I'll just check my email to make sure there's nothing too pressing, and then I'll get to the important stuff." And the next thing you know, two hours have gone by, you haven't gotten to any of the important stuff, and the rest of your day is crowded with meetings and calls.

Do the important stuff first.

The email can wait.

Honestly — how often have you received an email that couldn't have waited two hours for a response? If your answer is "Well, it *has* happened," then set your timer for two minutes, during which you may skim your email for anything that's a genuine crisis. Assuming there isn't one, go ahead and spend the next two hours on the important stuff.

Important stuff is the work that only you can do. It's the work that yields long-term benefits. It includes any creative work, any educational or self-improvement work, strategic thinking about projects or business, planning, relationship building, developing new material, staying on top of accounting and administrative systems, and dreaming up new ways to spread the good word about your work.

If you commit to spending the first two hours of your day on your important stuff, I guarantee that your overall productivity will go way, way up. I will also bet that once your team knows that you don't respond to every little tiny request immediately, they'll start figuring stuff out for themselves. Heck, they might even stop bothering you with the small stuff entirely.

> The important stuff is the work that only you can do.

Communicate Promptly, but Not Necessarily Immediately

I usually wait four to twenty-four hours to respond to emails, calls, texts, and private messages. I find that this gives me time to prioritize, to consider people's requests, and to give them a solid answer, either yes or "No, but thank you so much for thinking of me." It's good to be a bit elusive, I think. Be reliable, but not infinitely available.

Consume News Consciously

I love our global connectedness. I love staying abreast of trends and learning about the world. I consider it part of my civic responsibility to stay up on current events.

For me, the best way to get the news is from a good, old-fashioned newspaper. Does that mean that I am usually learning about the world's latest violent action the day after it happened? Absolutely. I prefer it that way. I have to be careful what images I allow into my brain, because I can never get them out. I'm not really interested in live coverage of the latest car chase, mass shooting, or political dustup. I find discretion really is the better part of valor, and being able to learn about the world's events at my own speed — not as dictated by the ceaseless twenty-four-hour news cycle — helps make me a calmer, more peaceful person.

> Be careful what images you allow into your brain, because you can never get them out.

The purpose of a news show is to keep you watching the news. The news — whether it's on radio, TV, or online — is entertainment. It is written and produced in a way intended to keep you engaged and emotionally stimulated. This means that the people reading and commenting on the news are entertainers. No matter how highbrow (or lowbrow, for that matter) they may seem, they are acting out a story for you. That's why they structure the news the way they do, and why they run those teasers. (In your best news-announcer voice, say this: "Scissors. They cut things. Will they cut you? Find out at eleven!" Or, "Stay tuned and find out which popular TV star just got a haircut that could change everything!" Now make up your own.)

I invite you to take a look at the amount of time you spend on this kind of entertainment (known in my house as *info-ad-u-edu-tain-u-ment*). Examine the voices you are allowing to influence your opinions, and consider whether the thoughts you have about current events are your own. When you let other people — particularly people in the entertainment industry — form your opinions for you, or tell you what's important, you give away your power.

Seek Out New Media

We are fortunate to live in a time when artists are able to control the means of distributing their work. We don't need to wait for a record label to discover the next great jazz musician and deliver a CD to our local store. The jazz musician can put her music out into the world all by herself, in her own way, and you can get it straight from the source. Better yet, you can engage in a conversation with her, and with her other fans, who, since they clearly share your excellent taste, will probably be people you'll enjoy getting to know.

There are so many wonderful, quirky, interesting, and uplifting pieces of art, writings, music, podcasts, games, movies, puzzles, blogs, novels, poems, craft projects, meditations, videos, and lectures available right on your laptop that you need never be constricted by mass-market entertainment again — unless you want to, because there is some terrific mass-market stuff out there, too.

You no longer need to live in a big city to experience diversity. Culture is everywhere, and not just "high" culture. You can so easily find out about whatever interests you — whether it's deep-sea fishing or Maori tattoos or carving radishes into roses. The human community is telling stories, and it is our privilege to listen.

Refuse to be bored.

Get out of your rut. Doing, watching, or listening to the same things every day makes time feel like it's slipping right through your fingers. On the other hand, the hours you spend learning and enjoying great culture will enrich your days and enliven your nights. Give yourself some new memories.

Write *Everything* Down in Your Calendar

Schedule your morning walk. Schedule your visit with a dear friend. Schedule your summer vacation, your trip to see the family (because spending time with family, while enjoyable in its own way, is not a vacation and should not be treated as such). Schedule your reading time, your clearing off your desk time, and your flea-market browsing time. If you put it in your calendar, you increase the chances that you will actually do it a thousandfold.

I hear from people all the time, "I wish I had time to write a book." You do. You are just spending that time on other things. So if you want to write a book, start putting it down as an unmissable appointment. Decide that there's no such thing as writer's block, sit down, and put words on paper. They don't have to be good words. In fact, they probably won't be. But you can't make it better if you never start. And you can't start if you never set aside the time.

> You can't make it better if you never start.

I still keep a datebook, because I have yet to find a better technology. I find paper and pen to be easy to use and reliable, with the added benefit that once I've written something down, I am much more likely to remember it. I can also leave myself important visual clues when I mark my calendar by hand.

For example, today's entry has the word *write* in tall, stretched-out letters that take up the whole area in order to cue me that I shouldn't even think about doing anything else today. Tomorrow is Friday, and I have a big *X* through the last part of the day. I don't like to work on Friday afternoons, so I block out that time each week to play hooky. Yes. I actually schedule my goofing-off time. Because if I didn't schedule it, I would be sitting at my desk, not really working but not really enjoying the free time, either. Being in that gray area is neither productive nor restful, and I suspect it's why so many people feel burned out. They don't experience the energy surge that comes with doing good work or the recharge of really walking away from work for a while.

I also maintain a Google calendar because my team needs access to my schedule, but I can't say I refer to it very often. Either way — analog or digital — experiment until you find a system that you enjoy using so that you actually use it.

Caution: this calendaring activity might trigger your inner teenage rebel. "No way, man," you think, "I need my freedom! I'm not going to be tied down. I just want to go wherever the day takes me." I know the feeling. But examine, for a moment, the results that strategy has gotten you. If you're getting everything done and enjoying plenty of free time and you're not constantly stressed out that you might have forgotten something important, then congratulations, you can skip this suggestion. But chances are, you are not really enjoying your freedom. Chances are, you are feeling chaotic and always running a bit behind. Give this writing it down in the calendar thing a try. I think you'll find that when you schedule your playtime, as well as your work time, you get to enjoy both.

Structure is freedom.

LITTLE CHANGES ACTION STEP: Pick a heretofore neglected activity that's important to you and put it in your calendar. No backing out, even if it starts to seem impractical later on, okay?

7. ➡ Quit Playing Overwhelmed Poker

HAVE YOU NOTICED that there's a worldwide game of "overwhelmed poker" going on? It sounds like this:

Person 1: "I'm so overwhelmed. I had to get up at 6 AM to work on my presentation and then corral the kids, race to my client meeting, get across town for a luncheon, and now I won't get home until after 7 PM."

Person 2: "Oh, me, too. I'm sooooooo busy it's really overwhelming. I actually had to get up at 5 AM to finish my new client proposal, and then I had all these meetings, and then of course there's the big project I'm in charge of, and I can't possibly leave work until at least 8 PM."

Person 3: "You two are so lucky. I'm *so* much busier than both of you..."

It's time to drop the glorification of overwhelm. Busy is not a virtue. You don't get bonus points for being stressed out, exhausted, and depleted. Plus I think you're short-changing yourself by using *overwhelmed* as a catchall word.

> Drop the glorification of overwhelm. Busy is not a virtue.

Saying that you feel overwhelmed is about as useful as telling the doctor that you feel tired. It's not that it's not true, it's just that there are too many root causes of tiredness for it to be helpful in diagnosis. There are

40

a lot of different ways to be overwhelmed, and each of them needs a slightly different cure.

Here are nine of the ways I've found:

- too many ideas
- too many half-finished projects
- too many intermediate steps
- actually, underwhelmed
- buying groceries at the Quickie Mart
- Cantsayno syndrome
- too much time / no deadline
- time boulders
- overwrought because of chronic overcomplication

In the following sections we'll look at each of these one at a time.

LITTLE CHANGES ACTION STEP: Stop saying you're overwhelmed. If you must refer to your activity level, at least try something a bit more amusing. My grandmother used to say she was "busier than a one-armed paper hanger." Or make up an expression of your own, like "Too many baskets, only one burro." Take responsibility by saying, "I've chosen to keep my schedule quite full this week," or admit that you kind of relish it by saying, "I'm in the deep end of the pool with no floaties this week, and while I'm having fun paddling, it's not leaving me time for anything extra."

8. ➡ You're Overwhelmed Because You Have Too Many Ideas

ONE OF THE PROBLEMS my creative clients experience is a surfeit of ideas. No sooner do they have one, vivid, glorious, full-blown idea (which, in and of itself, overwhelms them, because how could you even begin moving forward on such a big idea?) than they have another and another.

Should you create a gallery show featuring the photographs you took at the end of your grandfather's life? Or move to Oregon and open a yoga studio? But you've always wanted to publish your poetry, too.... You can see how a person could get immobilized, watching brilliant ideas shoot across their mind one after the other, like falling stars.

If you are this kind of a person, you have a beautiful, fertile mind. (Please tell me that you've found yourself a line of work where this quality is appreciated.)

Start writing these ideas down. You don't need to commit to any of them, but you can start enjoying the flow of innovation. After all, not every idea is meant to be acted on. Also, once you start writing your ideas down, you might realize that some of them are recurring, and you can take the persistence of the idea as a sign of its vigor. Or seeing them all together, you might notice that some ideas could be combined. For example, you might find that making a short Ken Burns–style film or slideshow featuring your photographs with you reading your poems as a voice-over might create something poignant and wonderful. Who knows, maybe you could even play it as a closing meditation when you teach yoga in Oregon.

Stop thinking that you have too many ideas and start appreciating and managing your ideas instead. You may find that taking the pressure off makes it easier to turn some of those ideas into reality.

LITTLE CHANGES ACTION STEP: Start writing down all of your ideas, no matter how far-fetched, foolish, or plain-Jane they may seem. Next, find a good place to store them all. I like to use those cardboard magazine holders as a kind of stand-up vertical file, but accordion file folders, large envelopes, and old tea tins work fine, too. Or perhaps you'll prefer an online solution. Whatever works for you is what's best.

9. ➡ Completion Is Overrated

THERE'S A HALF-COMPLETED SWEATER in the knitting basket. There's the first three chapters of a novel in a drawer. There are the specialty tools that you bought to make the ornaments for Baby's First Christmas, even though Baby is now entering the fifth grade.

When you see a reminder of something you've left undone everywhere you look, you are automatically going to feel exhausted. Half-completed tasks create what the productivity guru David Allen calls "open loops" in your mind, and those open loops take up a lot of bandwidth.

There are plenty of good reasons to have stopped moving forward on a project. You might have simply lost interest. That's fine. There are no starving creatives in Antarctica being deprived because you didn't finish what's on your plate, so to speak.

You might have stopped because you made a mistake or hit a wall, and your misguided perfectionism won't let you keep going. This could be a good time to make some 5-Minute Art about that perfectionist voice and see if you can't liberate your project from her thorny clutches. It's not like there's *really* a right way to do creative things.

Fear of commitment can sometimes play a role, too. Allowing yourself to get too deep into a project might mean that it's actually important to you, and it might have a real impact on your life, your work, and your relationships. So you keep it casual. Being a creative Casanova might feel like it's protecting your heart, but ultimately you're setting yourself up for dissatisfaction. What do you suppose might happen if you committed fully to your work?

I've also seen people quit mid-project because they find themselves in what the master consensus facilitator Sam Kaner calls the Groan Zone. He uses this expression to describe the point in consensus facilitation where diverse opinions have been expressed, and it feels like you've reached an impasse and will never find common ground — which is often the moment right before some new and beautiful solution emerges. I find it works equally well to refer to the sloggy middle of any project. Once that new-project smell has worn off and the end seems too far away, it's easy to let boredom and discouragement take the wheel. Try creating some minigoals, or even microgoals, and make sure you're rewarding yourself for your incremental progress.

LITTLE CHANGES ACTION STEP: Have a frank conversation with your inner, wise self about one of your half-done projects, and make a swift decision either to let it go or to schedule time in your calendar so you can get back to work on it.

10. → Feel Free to Leapfrog

WAITING MY TURN IN THE GROCERY LINE, I noticed a tabloid headline that said, "Comedy Star Loses 50 Pounds and Finds Love!" Now, I'm delighted for this star's happy news, but that headline implies that if a person — even a TV star — wants to find love, they should probably lose weight first. And that's just silly. You can find love at any size, age, or station in life. And putting a bunch of incremental steps in between where you are and the place you want to go is a surefire strategy for overwhelm.

I've also heard circular excuses like "Well, I would update my website, but I need a new photo, which means I need a new shirt, which means I need to find that gift card to the department store that I got three years ago, because heaven knows I don't have any spare cash lying around, because I don't have enough clients, because my website's not updated..." Have you experienced merry-go-round thinking like this?

> You can find love at any size, age, or station in life.

Other discouraging "intermediate step" thoughts can include believing that:

- you need a degree or certification
- you need to wait until your kids are older
- you want to wait until you can afford better equipment

- it's too soon to start something new after a heartbreak or disappointment
- you feel the irresistible impulse to research, research, research
- you need to pay your dues first
- you need to intern or work for free to get experience

Take my word for it: you know more than you think you know, and you will never be more ready than you are right now.

LITTLE CHANGES ACTION STEP: What if you could just leapfrog right to your destination? What would that look like? What could you attempt? Write it down.

11. ➤ Actually, You're Underwhelmed

SOMETIMES YOU FEEL OVERWHELMED not because something is hard or complicated, but rather because you simply don't want to do it.

My dear friend Amy Ahlers, the "Wake-Up Call Coach," was the one who first introduced me to the idea that sometimes people will say that they are overwhelmed when, actually, they are underwhelmed.

Remember the last time you had a bunch of fiddly little things that needed doing? Did you get that feeling of being exhausted and annoyed before you even started? Yep. That's being underwhelmed.

> Sometimes people will say that they are overwhelmed when, actually, they are underwhelmed.

Or maybe you've got a project that seems okay, and it presses on you because you feel like it needs to be done, but you just can't get excited about it.

Jacob had a pretty good personal-training business going. He was as busy as he wanted to be with his Hollywood clientele, and his income was stable. But gradually he noticed himself slipping. He would neglect to invoice his clients, which hurt his finances, and he found himself just going through the motions with some of his long-time customers. He kept saying that it was happening because he was just "overwhelmed." Nope. He was suffering from a classic case of underwhelm. He was bored. And he was about to bore himself right out of business.

A bit more investigation revealed that the reason Jacob was bored was that he had achieved a level of excellence in his business — both the training he offered and in his behind-the-scenes business systems — and he needed a new challenge. We made a list of a few ideas: offering a new type of class, which could be fun, or starting to teach online, thus opening him up to an international following. But the idea that got Jacob all lit up was the idea of teaching other struggling trainers the marketing and sales system he had developed over the years for getting, keeping, and wowing high-end clients. Now Jacob has two businesses, both booming, and neither is overwhelming.

LITTLE CHANGES ACTION STEP: What's underwhelming you? Could you find someone else to do it? Or could you turn it into a game? Is there a way to raise the stakes in order to make it more interesting? Rather than having to raise $1,000 for the library fund, what if you made it $10,000, or $100,000? Does that seem like a juicier project?

12. ➟ Quit Buying Groceries at the Quickie Mart

WHEN PEOPLE TALK TO ME about not having enough time in their day, I usually find some combination of these misjudgments:

- not being realistic about how much time some tasks actually take
- not prioritizing activities, or allowing priorities to shift
- failing to think things through, not planning ahead

When you are not realistic with yourself about how much time something actually takes, you feel rushed. And when you fail to prioritize your activities, you end up spending way too much time on the wrong things and don't have nearly enough time for the right things.

When you fail to plan ahead, you end up scrambling around at the last minute, and often the results are unsatisfactory.

For example, maybe you often don't remember that you've got to make dinner until you're on your way home, forcing you to grab whatever groceries you can find at the local Quickie Mart. Instead, take the time to put those responsibilities into your schedule right along with your other commitments. Too often your personal tasks end up being crammed into the corners of your day, and then you are forced to rush, which just adds to your feelings of being overwhelmed.

Remember to account for transit time: getting-stuck-in-traffic time, finding-a-parking-place time and waiting-for-the-elevator time. Failing to account for the time it takes to get from one place to another is a leading cause of pernicious lateness, and it is one of the hallmarks of the permanently overwhelmed.

By the same token, do yourself a favor and remember to build in ten or fifteen minutes of buffer time before and after phone calls and meetings so you have time to breathe, get a drink of water, collect your thoughts, and move calmly into the next scheduled activity.

LITTLE CHANGES ACTION STEP: Take ten minutes and try writing out every bit of your schedule for the whole day, not just the big chunks. This exercise may seem tedious, but I find that writing out how I am actually spending my time and being realistic about what one person can get done in a given period is a lot less stressful than imagining that I can, say, get showered, dressed, and coiffed for a meeting in less than seventeen minutes.

You know, I used to compress my "getting ready" time so much that I was tearing around like a crazy person every time I had to get out the door. I never compromised my travel time — I was always punctual. But I would delay and delay getting myself ready until I had no choice but to throw on the first outfit I tried on and then do my makeup in the car. Finally I realized that this self-sabotaging pattern was my way of using adrenaline as a boost to get me out the door. You see, I am a total homebody: I never really want to go anywhere. On the other hand, I refuse to be late. So I would watch the clock until I had just barely (but not really) enough time and then use the rush of panic to fuel my departure. Once I realized what I was doing, I gradually started moving back the moment I considered the last possible minute for leaving so that I had time to put on makeup in front of the mirror, check the directions to where I was going, grab a bottle of water, and attend to all those other details that make life more pleasant. (By the way, it's actually illegal in some states to apply makeup while driving, so let's all promise that we won't do that anymore.)

13. ➡ Cantsayno Syndrome

ARE YOU THE PERSON EVERYONE CALLS when they need something? Are you asked to be on every committee and every advisory board? Do you often find yourself letting people "pick your brain" or call you "just to vent"? If so, you may be suffering from Cantsayno syndrome.

Cantsayno syndrome causes its victims to agree to things they don't want to do, be accommodating to those who don't deserve it, and to fail utterly at putting themselves and their own work first. Symptoms include a stomach in knots, beleaguered sighs, and the deep-seated concern that if you were to say no, people wouldn't like you anymore.

We're tribal animals. We are very sensitive to the needs of the group because we know that we cannot survive alone. As much as we might wish everyone would just go away sometimes, our animal brain tells us that we must stay in the good graces of the group, or we will die. So most of the behavior that you might call people pleasing is part of your excellent survival mechanism. You don't want to be perceived as being greedy or selfish, or taking up too many resources — that might get you kicked out of the group. You want to be well liked. You want to contribute as much as you can to the tribe. That's just good sense.

It's not low self-esteem that's got you trapped, and it's not that you're a wimp. You are just letting your survival mechanism run the show when your survival is not actually at stake.

You were raised to be a nice person. You were raised to share your toys, keep your voice down, and not snatch the frosting off your birthday cake and eat it with your bare hands. Guess what? It worked. All that socializing worked. You are a very nice person. So you can stop proving it all the time.

Right now, the way you constantly monitor your behavior is like rereading the driver's manual every time you get in the car. Not every moment of your life has to be a testament to your niceness. You can afford to be a bit not-nice, to keep your toys to yourself, to yell and scream a bit, and to make a mess of that cake. Go for it.

> All that socializing worked. You are a very nice person.

If you stop giving your life over to whatever person or organization is sucking you dry, you'll find that they won't actually throw you out, and even if they do throw you out, it will probably feel like a relief. Either way, I'm pretty confident you won't be put out on an ice floe.

If it feels like too big a stretch to simply decline, you can try this: the next time someone asks you to do something that you don't want to do, just tell them that I won't let you. Yep. Just say, "Oh, gosh, Jerry, I would love to help run rehearsals for the talent show, but I'm working with this consultant named Sam, and she just will not let me take on any additional projects. If it were up to me, I would be happy to do it, of course, but I daren't — Sam would just have my head."

See? Easy. Make me the heavy.

LITTLE CHANGES ACTION STEP: Politely decline something today.

14. ⟶ Minimum Daily Requirement

You think that once you get that big expanse of time, you're going to be in clover. You're going to get all those projects done around the house, you're going to finally have time to write, do yoga, and practice the flute, and it's going to be great. Retirement. Getting laid off. Summer vacation.

And then that big expanse of time comes, and somehow, day after day, the time slips by, and you just don't get anywhere.

Having too much time can make a project feel just as overwhelming as not having enough time. When you can start anytime, how do you know when to start?

The other problem with this problem is that no one believes it's a problem. You feel ungrateful at best and like a fool at worst complaining that you have too much time. Who's going to sympathize with that? So you keep it to yourself. And you feel ashamed. And nothing feeds shame like secrecy. Can you see how a person could end up in a downward spiral that leads straight to long afternoons spent watching home-remodeling shows?

Now, I love home-remodeling shows, but I also believe that we are naturally inclined toward productivity. We love to be learning, doing, and playing. We love to stretch and grow and solve problems, and we love to feel like we're making a contribution to the world. Too much unstructured time can be stressful and depressing. When we don't know what to do with ourselves, we give up.

The trick is to inject some creative tension into your life. The word *tension* gets a bad rap, but remember that it is structural tension that holds the keystone in every arch — and sexual tension is often the beginning of all kinds of wonderful things.

Think of a goal that frightens you a little bit, something that stirs you up, maybe even something that you're pretty sure is impossible. Let it loom large in your mind. Connect with it. Feel the energetic relationship — the tension — between where you are now and where the goal is. Feel that energetic spoke of the Net between you and that goal, and let that tension pull you forward into taking one first step.

When you've taken one step, celebrate. It's easy to brush aside first steps, especially when you believe that you really should be farther along already, but don't. You did something, which is more than you did yesterday. Which is excellent. Be proud.

Now create a "minimum daily requirement" (MDR) for yourself. Make it something super-easy to do but still meaningful. If you want to write a book, perhaps your MDR is to write one sentence on an index card. If you're trying to declutter the garage, maybe you will commit to spending five minutes a day in there, whether you do any work or not. And of course there's my favorite "fifteen minutes a day" strategy. I firmly believe that spending just fifteen minutes a day on the project that is dearest to your heart has the power to change your entire life. Try it and let me know.

If your project is a bit epic, you can do yourself a favor by setting a series of six-week minigoals that will lead you to that bigger result. Six weeks is enough time to see significant progress, and two six-week periods will take you through a season. To create a plan in which, say, you research your historical novel in the fall, begin writing at the winter solstice, and have a rough first draft by spring might have a nice, natural rhythm to it.

By allowing yourself to engage with a big, juicy project, create incremental six- and twelve-week goals, and maintain your minimum daily requirement, you can shake yourself out of the shadowy morass of too much time and right into the sunny fields of creative productivity.

LITTLE CHANGES ACTION STEP: Write down a goal that sends a genuine thrill through your body. Now write down what you think a good minimum daily requirement for achieving that goal might be. Your MDR should be so small that there's no way you *can't* do it. Now reduce that MDR by half. That's right — lower the bar. So if you want to get in shape and your initial MDR is to do fifty sit-ups a day, reduce that number to twenty-five. If you want to redo the backyard, then commit to spending just fifteen minutes a day out there. Of course, you may end up doing fifty sit-ups or spending all afternoon weeding, but that's a bonus. You still do your MDR the next day.

Steady, consistent movement is how the Colorado River carved out the Grand Canyon, and that same persistence will give you equally awe-inspiring results.

15. ➡ Time Boulders

Stercus accidit [Life happens].
— DAVID HUME

SOMETIMES THINGS JUST HAPPEN. Big, attention-consuming, time-demanding, energy-eating things. A new baby in the house. A health crisis — your own, or one affecting someone dear to you. A demanding full-time job. A serious financial setback. These are real-life things that cannot be delegated or ignored.

I call these big life events "time boulders" because they appear to sit like giant rocks in the road to your future. They appear immovable, impenetrable, and permanent.

This is an illusion. Time boulders are temporary. You know this, because everything is temporary.

The mantra "It has come to pass" can be quite useful during these times. And I like to say it with a little pause in the middle, so it sounds like "It has come...to pass." In other words, the reason it has come is so that it can pass. And remembering that it *will* pass can help me find and cherish the lesson that has been custom-designed for me by this challenging episode.

Here are a few tips for getting through those "life happens" times.

1. Put self-care at the top of your list. Now more than ever, you need to be as rested and nurtured as you can possibly be. You need all your strength. Double up on your massage appointments, go for your annual physical, and make sure you have time for breathing, prayer, or meditation as well as at least fifteen minutes a day of walking, dancing, swimming, or other fun physical activity. Put your oxygen mask on first so that you can help others.

It has come…to pass.

2. *Get help.* It's easy to feel like you have to shoulder the whole burden, but that's a falsehood. Write out all the tasks that need to get done. Put your initials by the ones that can only be done by you, and delegate the rest. For example: only you can hold the hand of your beloved in the hospital, but someone else can cook dinner. Only you can do your creative work, but someone else can make plane reservations and book a hotel. Only you can go on job interviews, but someone else can pick up the kids from school. I know, you believe that another person won't do as good a job as you would, but you might be surprised. And remember: this is only temporary.

3. *Find a safe place to share your feelings.* When you are in a crisis, you are living in a slightly different reality from everyone else, and it's easy to feel alone and misunderstood. Please seek out a trusted adviser, a trained professional, or a support community with whom you can share the truth about what's happening without feeling judged or like you're hurting anyone's feelings by being truthful. Even "wonderful" time boulders, like a wedding or a new baby, will bring moments of exhaustion, frustration, sorrow, and anger, and those feelings need to be felt if you're going to move through them.

This seems like as good a time as any to tell you that in 1988, when I was twenty years old, I was in a car accident that was no one's fault. I broke my back, shattering my twelfth thoracic vertebra, and fractured my skull in two places. I spent several weeks in the hospital, and I had to learn to walk again. Once I got home, I had a long recovery time, during which I couldn't do much on my own. Aside from the pain I was in, and the frustration I felt at my new physical limitations, I felt very alone. My twentysomething friends couldn't exactly relate to what I was experiencing.

But I had a friend named Joe, who was dying of AIDS. He, too, had been healthy and robust just a few months earlier, and together we groused about doctors, painkillers, and feeling so helpless. We made horrible, hilarious, gallows-humor jokes about his condition and dirty, you-had-to-be-there jokes about mine.

I remember calling him up the day I could finally put on my own socks. (Putting on your own socks while you're strapped into a huge back brace is tougher than it sounds.) He was so happy for me, and I was so glad to have one person in my life with whom to celebrate my milestone. After we hung up, I cried my eyes out, because I was getting better, and Joe was not.

I think of Joe often, and I am so grateful that I had someone so honest, so compassionate, and so funny in my life with whom to share that experience. (One time he told me that I should be careful if I ever had phone sex so that I wouldn't get — wait for it — hearing aids. We just about wet our pants laughing at that one.)

4. *Acknowledge that your story has changed.* We all tell ourselves stories about our lives and the roles we play.

"I'm a successful businessperson and a terrific tennis player."

"I'm the older sister who's married and the 'responsible' one."

"I'm the life of the party!"

It's easy to confuse those stories with our true identity. So when suddenly we can no longer play tennis, or we're no longer married, or we find that the party has turned into a teeny-tiny substance-abuse problem, we become afraid that our whole personality might unravel. But this is a wonderful opportunity to make some 5-Minute Art to better understand your old story and your new story as it unfolds. You are always you, and the qualities that made you a great athlete, a wonderful wife, and a fun person will always be with you.

5. Make a date with your other goals. You may feel that as you are dealing with your time boulder, some of your other goals need to be set aside. That's perfectly natural, and might even be true. But before you throw your projects out with the bathwater, ask yourself if continuing to work on your goal — even for just five minutes a day — might actually help you move through this complicated time. If the answer is yes, then please claim that time. If you truly feel like it needs to wait, then just set that other goal or project gently on the shelf and mark the date when you will pick it back up. So you might put your portfolio in a folder and make a note in your calendar to begin sketching again on the Monday after your birthday, or on the kids' first day of school. Making the conscious decision either to continue working or to quit for the moment will keep the flame alive.

6. Look for the lesson. As the wise woman says, "This is not happening to you. It is happening for you." No matter how dismal your current circumstance may seem, it can be worth it to ask, "What am I being asked to learn here?" You may be getting a graduate degree in forgiveness, or in patience. Maybe you're being called forward to be a better son or daughter, a better employee, or a better boss. You may be getting the opportunity to learn about living with a disability, negotiating with creditors, or navigating government assistance programs. The true meaning of this part of your journey may not be revealed until many years from now, but staying aware that there is a lesson and that it is for your greater good might be a useful perspective to hold.

7. Surrender. I sometimes think that dealing with the "life happens" stuff is like standing waist-deep in the ocean. You

> No matter how dismal your current circumstance may seem, it can be worth it to ask, "What am I being asked to learn here?"

know how you need to both stand firm *and* let yourself get pushed by the waves a bit in order not to get knocked over? Sometimes the water is flat and it's easy. On those days you can feel almost "normal." And sometimes a huge wave will come out of nowhere and surprise you and tumble you and spit you out on the sand, frightened and disoriented. Do what you can do. Accept your limitations even as you strive to exceed them. You are always doing the best you can do. So is everyone else. Surrender is not giving up; surrender is giving in.

> Surrender is not giving up; surrender is giving in.

LITTLE CHANGES ACTION STEP: Spend fifteen minutes on something that is important only to you. Preferably right now.

16. ➡ You're Not Overwhelmed,
You're Overwrought

YOUR FEELINGS OF OVERWHELM arise because you have an entrancingly subtle mind. You see the infinite possibilities and permutations of every idea. To settle on just one idea feels cruel and unusual. Life is about feelings and ideas. It cannot be rushed. It happens in the gray area. You love all of your ideas, and to pick just one feels like you're going to hurt the other ideas' feelings. It's like choosing your favorite child.

Plus, forcing yourself to decide — on anything, really — makes you feel like someone is taking away your freedom, and you hate to be fenced in.

Yep. I get it. And it's perfectly reasonable to have an adverse reaction to the word *decide*. After all, the root of the word is the Latin *cide*, which means "to cut" or "to kill." It's the same root that we see in the words *homicide* and *pesticide*. By choosing to focus on one goal or project, you may feel like you are killing off all other possibilities.

I might suggest that school has kind of messed with your head, too. Because in school, the way you succeed on a test is by knowing the answers in advance. But life is not like that. In life, and in the creative process, the whole point is that you do not know the answers in advance. Heck, you may not even know the questions. So all you can do is trust your intuition and follow the sparkly bread crumbs. Think of your life as an adventure to be lived, not an exam on which you need to get a perfect score.

> Trust your intuition and follow the sparkly bread crumbs.

You feel overwhelmed because you are a sensitive person, and you are vibrating with all the possibilities of life. That's fine. Just remember that not everything needs to be fraught with meaning, and it's okay to take small steps, to experiment, and to play around. You may have a native mistrust of anything that seems too simple or too easy, but give it a try.

LITTLE CHANGES ACTION STEP: Challenge yourself to take only the simplest, easiest, most affordable next step toward something that feels overwhelming. Make sure it takes less than fifteen minutes and is easily within your budget. Notice how you feel and what results you get. Do this every day for a week, and see how events unfold. Also, you might enjoy reading the "You might be a creative person if..." checklist at www.StartRight WhereYouAre.com.

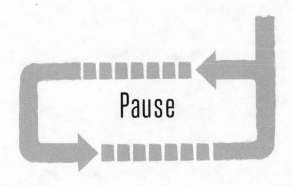

Pause

All I Have

Dear God,

All I have I submit to you.
All I am is created by you.
All I will be I dedicate to you.
I humble my heart to walk your path.
I submit gracefully to your will.
I feel your hand on my shoulder, your breath in my breath.
My trust in you is absolute.
Help me hear you — every little whisper.

Love,
Me

17. ➡ Reimagining Well-Being

As WE CONTINUE TO EXAMINE the assertion "Nothing is more important than your well-being," the question arises, "What does 'your well-being' look like?" I find the standard women's-magazine examples of *well-being* and *self-care* to be unimaginative and often not applicable. Some of us find getting a manicure to be more of an annoyance than a treat.

So let's start with what your version of *well-being* feels like. What words connote *well-being* to you? Make a list.

Here are 128 to get you started:

active	bouncy
adventurous	bright-eyed and bushy-tailed
alit	calm
animated	cheerful
aroused	chipper
at ease	comfortable
athletic	contented
at home	cool as a cucumber
beaming	delighted
beautiful	deserving
blessed	devil-may-care
blissful	dreamy
blithe	eager

ecstatic
elegant
evangelical
even-tempered
fine
fit as a fiddle
friendly
frisky
giggly
glad
good-humored
grateful
hale and hearty
handsome
happy
healthy
in control
in fine fettle
ingenious
inquisitive
insightful
intuitive
in tune
joking
jovial
joyous
jumpy
kind
knowing
kooky
laid-back
laughing

listening
lively
loving
low-key
lucky
magical
meditative
merciful
middle-of-the-road
mindful
mischievous
naive
naked
natural
nice
noble
oblivious
observant
of consequence
on cloud nine
open-minded
part of the Net
peaceful
perspicacious
placid
playful
pleased
potent
powerful
prayerful
prosperous
purring

queenly	sunny
quiescent	sweet-tempered
quiet	thankful
rebellious	tickled pink
replete	tranquil
resilient	tricky
robust	turned on
safe	unhurried
safe and sound	unworried
sensual	upbeat
serene	vivacious
sexy	well groomed
sharp as a tack	well made
snuggly	whole
spaced out	wise
spicy	xenodochial (friendly to strangers)
spontaneous	Zen
stretched	zesty
strong	zippy

Want to experiment more? An expanded, downloadable version of this list is available at www.StartRightWhereYouAre.com.

LITTLE CHANGES ACTION STEP: Pick a few of the adjectives that feel particularly spot-on for you, write them down, and keep them in a place where you will see them again.

18. ➡ Activating Your Well-Being

NOW THAT WE KNOW how you want to feel, let's ask what activities give you those feelings. What things do you do that make you feel more you? Breathing, laughing, moving your body, singing, being quiet? Getting more than six hours of sleep? Taking a daily walk? Having time to read a romance novel? Spending time with friends? Take a look at the list below and see which ones call out to you.

You will notice that television, movies, cruising the internet, and video games are *not* a part of this list. While these activities can be pleasurable, they are mostly passive, and hence they have a tendency to anesthetize you rather than energize you.

Here are seventy ideas to get you started:

acting	crafting
attending a cultural event	dancing
boating	daydreaming
building	doing puzzles
canoeing	drawing
chanting	erotic play
clearing clutter	fine dining
coloring	gardening
composing	geocaching
cooking	getting a massage

getting lost
handcrafting
helping someone in need
hobbying
Hoverboarding
improvising
interviewing someone
inventing
jewelry designing
juggling
jumping rope
kite flying
knitting
language learning
lip-synching
martial arts
meditating
nature walking
needlework
organizing
origami
outlandish behavior
painting
people watching
photography
ping-pong
playing cards
playing laser tag
playing music
poetry
pottery
praying
quilting
reading
redecorating
running
sailing
skipping
spending time with animals
stand-up paddleboarding
studying / taking a class
surfing
swimming
tai chi
taking a bath
walking
wandering
writing
yoga
Zumba

LITTLE CHANGES ACTION STEP: Make a list of three activities that you suspect would promote your well-being and commit to doing one of them today.

19. ➡ In Search of a Fainting Couch

IN ADDITION TO FIGURING OUT what well-being means for you, it's important to learn what looks like "not-well-being" for you. How do you know when you are off track? What are your symptoms?

For me, not-well-being shows up as racing thoughts, also known as anxiety. (It's a little annoying that in the English language we use words like *anxiety* and *depression* to describe both a mood and a medical condition. So, just to be clear, I manage both the moods and the medical conditions of anxiety and depression.) And when my anxiety really kicks in — and it rarely does anymore, but when it does, it's a hurricane — I literally wring my hands. It's like I'm some eighteenth-century heroine in search of a fainting couch.

I used to try to make myself stop, but now I don't, because it's such an important signal to me. If I'm wringing my hands, I can notice that and think, "Oh, wow. I am super off-kilter. Something's really wrong. This is a really strong signal that I am not in my right mind." And it's a signal to the people who love me. My sister knows and Luke knows that if they see me wringing my hands, they should say, "Okay, she's a goner. Let's get her some water. Let's get her out of this situation."

Sometimes a symptom of not-well-being is not a physical behavior but rather a thought pattern. When depression creeps in, my first symptom is not being able to feel joy. So, for example, I might be out with friends, and I'll think to myself, "I can tell this is supposed to be fun, because I see other people laughing and smiling. I wonder why I am not experiencing the feeling of fun." That sensation is known as anhedonia: the inability to take pleasure in anything.

> When you are suffering from not-well-being, don't expect yourself to make any decisions. Don't even expect yourself to make a lot of sense.

Since we're on what I feel to be an underdiscussed subject, let me also name another symptom of a depressive episode, which is the certainty that the feeling is permanent. The depressed mind thinks, "Life is miserable, and I'm always going to be unhappy. I've always been unhappy, and I will always be unhappy. I can't even call to mind any time of happiness. Any happy memories feel false to me. I maybe thought I was happy, but I wasn't. Not really. And I can't imagine being happy in the future."

One of the horrible tricks that depression plays on you is to make you believe that it will never go away. Because when you're in it, you think, "This is never going to change. There is no hope for me." It's not so much that the pain is so bad as the conviction that it will never end. That's why depression can be a fatal disease.

Most of us have conditions that need to be managed: a tendency to overwork, to overdrink, to worry too much. Maybe you go on shopping sprees or get into a cycle of binging and purging. Maybe you hyperventilate or get vertigo or migraines. Maybe your back hurts. (Almost certainly your back hurts. Data from the National Institutes of Health indicate that eight out of ten people suffer back pain at some point in their lives. Maybe you don't feel anxiety because your back is feeling it for you.)*

---

* See "Back Pain," MedlinePlus, National Institutes of Health, www.nlm.nih .gov/medlineplus/backpain.html, accessed June 21, 2016.

Stay alert to the thoughts, behaviors, and aches and pains that let you know when you're off-kilter, and try to preprogram your response as you would if you were having a kind of allergic reaction. "Oh. There's my sign that I can't tolerate XYZ. I'm noticing that something is happening, my body is reacting, and I need to treat this reaction. I need to treat this episode."

Whatever your not-well-being symptom is, please don't criticize yourself for it. You've been doing the best you can. And now that you're going to be taking better care of yourself, perhaps that condition will lessen or even disappear.

But I want to be real here: life is a long road. My depression does occasionally come back, and when it does, I am reminded how my one-eyed therapist (I couldn't make this stuff up if I tried: I had a one-eyed therapist) told me, "When you have depression, you live in a house built on a cliff." At the time I got all sarcastic and said, "Well, thanks. That's inspiring." And she replied, "No. It's a neutral fact. Depression might always be with you. That yawning chasm might always be there, and it might always be a little dangerous for you." Now, years later, I find that her image reminds me to not get complacent.

These days, when depression does strike, I try to find the gift in it. I consider it an invitation to slow down. Since depression causes me to ruminate, I'll take the opportunity to examine my business, both its trajectory and its systems. After all, I'm in a pondering mood, so often I'll notice something that I wouldn't have been able to see if I were moving at my usual breakneck pace. I write more poetry. I make mordant jokes. I sleep more. I reread old books. And every day I push and poke at it a bit to see if I can get it to lift, even for a few hours. Because it has come...to pass.

But the best medicine is prevention. If you can acquaint

yourself with your own early warning signs, you may be able to head off those destabilizing moments and lessen their impact on your day.

LITTLE CHANGES ACTION STEP: Write down three behaviors or thought patterns that are symptoms of your not-well-being and share the list with someone you trust.

20. → HALTT

IN TWELVE-STEP PROGRAMS you learn the acronym *HALT*, which stands for "hungry, angry, lonely, tired." They suggest that if you are feeling bad, you first ask yourself if you are any of those things — hungry, angry, lonely, or tired — and then make fixing that condition your number one priority.

The addict is at risk of relapse when HALT takes hold, and the consequences for you, addict or not, can be equally destructive. Your thinking becomes muddy, and you become highly emotionally reactive. (Have you ever snapped at someone just because you forgot to eat lunch? Me too. Not my finest hour.)

When you're physically depleted, the lurking demons and monsters and bad thoughts get louder and feel more real. So you must fix the problem of being hungry, angry, lonely, and/or tired before you make any other decisions or try any other course of action.

And we might add a second *T* for "thirsty," because I once heard a Tim Ferris podcast in which he interviewed the motivational speaker Tony Robbins, and he asked, "Do you have any advice for people when they get discouraged?" Tony replied, "Stay hydrated," which I thought was quite astute.*

---

* "Tony Robbins on Morning Routines, Peak Performance, and Mastering Money," *The Tim Ferris Experiment*, October 15, 2016, fourhourworkweek.com/2014/10/15/money-master-the-game, accessed June 21, 2016.

LITTLE CHANGES ACTION STEP: Create a "HALTT Emergency Response" list. Decide what you might do the next time you find yourself overly hungry, angry, lonely, or tired. Putting a strategy in place before it happens can prevent a lot of damage. Keeping an energy bar in your bag to prevent low-blood-sugar meltdown or a squeezable stress ball on your desk to combat bureaucracy-induced rage might avert all kinds of unfortunate consequences. And heck, someday you might learn to rest before you get tired.

> You must fix the problem of being hungry, angry, lonely, and/or tired before you make any other decisions or try any other course of action.

Note: I know how easy it is to ignore the instruction to write out these examples of one thing or another. After all, this is probably not your first self-help rodeo — you're already pretty on to yourself. But do us both a favor and write it out anyway. You might surprise yourself. Want to write it on something fancy? You can download your own "HALTT Emergency Response" list at www.StartRightWhere YouAre.com.

21. ➤ Getting Out of the Urgency Trap

YOUR EMAIL PINGS. Your message app pings. Your other message app pings. You've got forty-seven notifications and thirteen new requests and an overflowing inbox. It all seems urgent. After all, it pinged. That must mean it's important.

Your brain is hardwired to respond to immediate stimulus. This is another survival mechanism. Anything that sounds like "Alert! Something is happening!" gives us a little hit of adrenaline, whether it's a rustle in the bush that indicates a hungry tiger is nearby or a text from the spouse reminding you to get milk on your way home.

Correspondingly, our brain releases a hit of the "feel-good" chemical dopamine each time we feel a sense of achievement, even if that achievement is simply texting back, "Yes. Milk. Love you." As Simon Sinek explains in his insightful book *Leaders Eat Last*, we can get addicted to the cycle of doing and doing and doing, and we fail to notice that nothing is actually getting done.

Bringing just a bit of mindfulness to your daily movements can help a lot. One way to check in with yourself is to play the Because/Because game.

The Because/Because game asks you to pause for one moment before you begin an activity and ask why you are doing what you're doing and why you're the person doing it.

So, in the moment before you start catching up with the

bookkeeping for your side hustle, you might have this conversation with yourself: "Why am I doing this bookkeeping? Because it's important to me that I know whether this side business is really profitable. Why am I the one doing this? Because even though I dislike doing these kinds of detail-oriented tasks, I'm the only employee." Now, this awareness might not lead you to hire an assistant immediately, but once you've had this conversation with yourself five times in a week, you might start to see the value of getting some help.

> We get addicted to the cycle of doing and doing and doing, and we fail to notice that nothing is actually getting done.

On the other hand, if you find yourself dreading a visit to Sad Susan, your friend who just ended yet another disastrous love affair, you might hear yourself thinking, "Why am I going to see Susan? Because she needs a shoulder to cry on. Why am I the one doing this? Because even though Susan's love life is a nonstop soap opera, I care deeply about her happiness." Remembering your true motivation can put a smile back on your face as you stop off along the way for the margarita mix and ice cream.

LITTLE CHANGES ACTION STEP: Put a few of your least favorite activities through the Because/Because game. Are there any that you could eliminate from your life today?

22. ➤ Your Well-Being

GO AHEAD AND SUMMARIZE your thinking about your own signs of well-being and not-well-being by writing out the answers to these questions swiftly, without pondering.

1. When you get stressed out, what are your warning signs?
2. What happens when you start to crumble and are not your best self?
3. How much time, money, and opportunity has crumbling cost you over time?
4. Do you express your stress physically?
5. Is there a new choice for your well-being that you can implement today?

LITTLE CHANGES ACTION STEP: Share these answers with someone in your life who cares about you.

23. ➤ Delegation for Recovering Perfectionists

LIKE MANY RECOVERING PERFECTIONISTS, I've found learning how to delegate to be a steep and rocky path. I truly believe that self-sufficiency is a virtue. And since my brain is so good at finding what it's looking for, I notice every single time that idea gets proved right, and so I always have lots of evidence for why it really is better if I just handle everything myself.

This kind of thinking, friends, is the devil in disguise.

My self-reliance came in handy when I was a latchkey kid in the seventies and in adulthood when I was an independent artist. Then, in the first years of running the Organized Artist Company, I found myself learning everything I could about websites, copywriting, graphic design, small business administration, webinars, teleclasses, and contracts and agreements, and then I really geeked out on internet and email marketing. Whenever one of my entrepreneurial friends complained about how her website was being held hostage by her designer, or how an assistant had screwed up the PPC (pay-per-click) ads again, I secretly felt very smug. At least if mistakes were made in my business, they were all mine.

Now this is where my vanity shows up — in not wanting others to know I made mistakes. If I had other people helping me, they would see my errors and misjudgments. Working alone, I could keep up a pretty good facade of shiny excellence.

But as the Organized Artist Company became increasingly successful, I realized I was doing a disservice to the people I was trying to serve by attempting to do everything myself. I was limiting my growth and the depth of my work. After all, the time I spent posting the webinar I'd just recorded was time I was not spending talking to new clients, developing new workshops, or writing books.

I had built a business with my own two hands, and I ended up with a business that I could hold in my own two hands. Cozy, but limited in scope.

Once I was willing to face down my ego and admit that my vision of self-sufficiency was a delusion and a trap, my business took a quantum leap forward, and revenue doubled. Little change, big difference.

> I built a business with my own two hands, and I ended up with a business that I could hold in my own two hands.

I realized that I had been listening too much to the complaints of other business-owner friends of mine about how hard it was to find good people. One friend was going through at least two new assistants a year. Each time she was convinced that the new person was the answer to her prayers, and each time she ended up disappointed. She didn't want to look at how her own behavior might be contributing to this cycle, so she just kept repeating it.

Once I turned my attention away from other entrepreneurs' tales of victimization and instead focused on the fact that I genuinely love working with other people, my team started to take shape. After all, I'd spent my entire life in the theater, and that's what theater, and particularly my subspecialty of improvisational theater, is all about — utter reliance on your fellows. I realized that I could hire people who shared my values, who would laugh at my jokes, and who had skills I couldn't even dream of. The next time I heard a friend singing the blues about an unreliable team member, I simply thought to myself, "That's not my story."

I have also used the thought "That's not my story" to fill events when everyone says it's impossible to fill an event these days, and to sell books when everyone says that publishing is dead. That may be their story, but it's not my story. Try it for yourself. "Change is hard"? That's not my story. "Teenagers are impossible"? That's not my story. "You can't get a well-paying job that's flexible"? That's not my story.

LITTLE CHANGES ACTION STEP: Write a five-minute fairy tale about one of your patterns. For example:

Once upon a time there was a clever queen who thought she had to do everything herself. One day while she was dusting the baseboards in the ballroom, her fairy godfather appeared to her and asked, "Why are you doing that, O Queen?" "It's so hard to get good help these days," said Queenie. He said, "Sweetheart, that isn't your story." Suddenly an army of handsome men appeared with feather dusters, and they had the whole ballroom cleaned in a jiffy. So that night, the queen hosted the first of many fabulous parties. As the music played and the conversation sparkled along with the champagne, Queenie was heard to say, "Ahh...now *this* is my story." It was rumored that later that night there was royal skinny-dipping. But that's another story.

24. ⟶ Hire Geniuses

THE MINUTE I OPENED MY EYES to the reality that I could hire geniuses and pay them well, geniuses came out of the woodwork. Here's one tip: never, ever skimp on talent. Cut back in other ways if you must, but high-quality people pay for themselves over and over again. Plus it feels good to be generous.

All of my team members have found me: I have never had to advertise for a position. Consider that for a moment. Are you leading your family, your group, your class, your team, or your organization in such a way that great people are automatically drawn to you? We'll talk more about tribes, teams, and values in chapter 59, but I wanted to mention it now to let the idea stew a bit.

Never, ever skimp on talent.

I often say, "The work only you can do, you must do. The work that someone else can do, someone else must do." Here's an example of that: I once had a friend who got a job working for a well-respected A-list celebrity. My friend was surprised to learn that this celebrity had a personal chef, a head housekeeper, a team of housemaids, a handyman, a chauffeur, several gardeners and pool maintenance people, a personal assistant, an assistant's assistant (that was my friend's job), a publicist, a stylist, a hair and makeup team, a social media manager, a decorator, a fitness trainer, and a life coach. This celebrity had outsourced almost everything in her life because, as she saw it, anyone could go shopping and pick up the dry cleaning and handle the details of the summer vacation to Maine, but only she could do her creative work and raise her children. So she didn't have a nanny or any in-house childcare. She felt that her job on this earth was to be a mom and be an actor. Everything else was outside her zone of genius.

If you're getting interrupted by a lot of not-important things and getting distracted all the time, you are being offered the opportunity to look at your priorities. There are probably quite a few daily activities that you can delegate, even if you don't have the household budget of a celebrity. Any repetitive activity or administrative process can be easily handed over, and, I promise, you will experience deep joy when you find someone to do the stuff you truly dislike doing, or weren't doing at all. And I know, they're not going to do it as well as you, but, honestly, who cares? Does what you're doing really have to be done as well as you're doing it? Does it really matter?

I know that feeling of, "Oh, it's going to take me four times longer to show them how to do it than it is for me to just do it myself." Yes, that's true, the first time, and maybe the second time and the third time and the fourth time. But by the fifth time, they'll be able to handle it themselves, and then you will never have to handle it again. Who knows, maybe they'll find an even better way to handle it.

Remember that delegation is not abdication. You don't get to hand things over and then never think about them again. You need to put processes in place so that the work is being checked and double-checked, though not necessarily by you. You must give your people both the responsibility and the authority for their projects. In other words, if you're going to delegate to a team member the task of sourcing 100-percent-recycled holiday cards to be printed and mailed to your whole client list by December 15, it will go much easier for you if you also give them the budget, the design parameters, and the timeline and then, other than checking in and double-checking at scheduled times, free them up to use their best judgment. The Ritz-Carlton hotels have famously empowered their employees to spend up to two thousand dollars per incident in order to solve a guest's problem. You may have noticed that customer-service people often have the responsibility to solve problems but not the authority to take any real action. By giving them both a budget and the authority to use it, the Ritz has ended up with faster problem solving and happier customers.

Finally, you will get much better results when you explain *why* you do things the way you do. So you might say, "Charlie, I'm putting you in charge of the holiday cards, and before we talk specifics, I want to explain to you a bit about the history of this project and how it's grown over the years, and why I've been doing it the way I've been doing it. It speaks to our values of heartfelt communication, so it's important that the card not look too 'canned,' and you know we also have a corporate value of 'reduce, reuse, recycle,' so we want to make sure it's as sustainable as we can."

Sharing the burden is sharing the wealth.

LITTLE CHANGES ACTION STEP: What's one recurring task you could delegate today? Bonus points awarded for actual delegation of said task.

25. ➡ Delegate It. Really. You Can Do This.

HERE ARE SOME GOOD REASONS to delegate something:

- It makes you tired when you even think about doing it.
- Allowing someone else to do it frees you up for activities that produce more income, more joy, or both.
- It's a simple or repetitive task.
- It would help another person to expand his or her skill set.
- It's not in your zone of genius.

Quickly jot down the answers to the following prompts:

- What's one task you would love to delegate?
- If you haven't delegated it up to now because of money, write down how much it would cost to pay someone else to do it.
- Write down three ways you could generate those funds. Think about funds that might come in if you didn't have to spend time on that task. In other words, if you didn't have to spend an hour a week editing your newsletter, you would have an extra hour in which to generate new business.
- If you haven't delegated this task up to now because of pride, or because you feel like no one else would do it properly, write down three words that describe how you might feel if someone else did it better than you.

- What do you think it would mean about you if you delegated this task?
- If you are still experiencing resistance to delegating, whose voice is in your head telling you it's wrong?
- What do you notice about how you are feeling now?

LITTLE CHANGES ACTION STEP: Answering these questions has probably led you to your next action step. So do that.

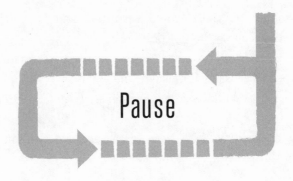

Pause

Another Person

Dear God,

I have worked myself into a lather.

I am sharing my work with another person soon, and it's causing me to lose my center. I feel jumpy.

I feel worried that I will fail, that I will blow this chance. I feel terrified that I might succeed and my life will change in ways I'm not comfortable with. And I'm most concerned that nothing will happen at all.

I'm making myself miserable by living in an imaginary future, God.

Help me to live in the present moment.

As I put my hand on my heart, let me feel the soft, quiet peace that is your now. Let me be filled with the certainty that if I stay connected to you,

I will see what is fun, funny, and joyful about this,

I will quit making nightmares in my mind,

I will focus my attention on this now right now.

Our one and only now.

Love,
Me

26. ➤ You're Not Thinking What You Think You're Thinking

WHEN IT COMES TO DECISION MAKING, we humans like to think that logic is our best and most reliable tool. But it turns out that we use logic a lot less than you might think.

Many of our daily decisions are really subconscious, "gut" decisions arrived at by a combination of instinct, feelings, and environmental triggers. For example, we decide whether or not someone is trustworthy within one-tenth of a second, according to a study at Princeton.* Then we cast around for some logical reason to back up our belief.

While traditional science has typically dismissed intuition as claptrap, there is increasing evidence suggesting that our intuition is actually a superfast, nonconscious act of pattern recognition, often leading to better decisions than logic alone.†

Even more challenging to the supremacy of logical thinking

---

* Janine Willis and Alexander Todorov, "First Impressions: Making Up Your Mind after a 100-Ms Exposure to a Face," *Psychological Science* 17, no. 7 (July 2006): 592–98, pss.sagepub.com/content/17/7/592.short?rss=1&s source=mfc.

† "Go With Your Gut: Intuition Is More Than Just a Hunch, Says New Research," *ScienceDaily*, 6 March 2008, www.sciencedaily.com/releases/2008 /03/080305144210.htm; see also the excellent books *Blink: The Power of Thinking without Thinking*, by Malcolm Gladwell (New York: Little, Brown, 2005), and *Thinking, Fast and Slow*, by the Nobel Prize winner Daniel Kahneman (New York: Farrar, Straus and Giroux, 2011).

is evidence that our thoughts aren't actually thoughts. A recent study published in the journal *Behavioral and Brain Sciences* seems to indicate that what we think of as "consciousness" or "thinking" is really just stimulus response.* When you see a thing, you think the thought you always think when you see that thing. When you see a person, you think the thought you always think when you see that person.

I recently visited an office where they kept a dish of candies on the reception desk. Although I am not a big fan of sweets, I cheerfully took one anyway. Because it was there. Those little foil-wrapped chocolate treats were just sitting there, and I ate one before I even thought about it.

And that dynamic, where you take action without really thinking about it, is the stimulus-response pattern that governs much of our behavior.

A study by Brian Wansink, the director of the Cornell University Food and Brand Lab and the author of *Slim by Design: Mindless Eating Solutions for Everyday Life*, found that people who kept their cereal boxes out on the kitchen counter weighed twenty-one pounds more than people who stored their cereal in the cabinet. One glimpse of the cereal box, and before you've even decided whether you're hungry, you're filling up a bowl. Next thing you know, you're consuming an extra two hundred calories a day and wondering why your favorite skinny jeans don't fit anymore.

And it's not just cereal boxes that can influence our behavior. In another famous study, people contributed 2.76 times more money to an honesty box in a coffee break room when an image of a face with eyes looking at them was taped to the refrigerator.

---

* Ezequiel Morsella, Christine A. Godwin, Tiffany K. Jantz, Stephen C. Krieger, and Adam Gazzaley, "Homing In on Consciousness in the Nervous System: An Action-Based Synthesis," *Behavioral and Brain Sciences* (June 2015), dx.doi.org/10.1017/S0140525X15000643.

Although it was unlikely that anyone could really see whether they gave money or not, the image of the eyes made people feel as though they were being watched, and thus they were more generous in their donations than they were during the weeks when the image on the fridge was of flowers.*

In what I think is a hilarious variation on this study, I remember seeing a video (which, regrettably, I couldn't find again in my research for this book), in which the unwitting subjects of the study contributed more to the coffee room's honesty box when there was a coconut on a shelf directly facing them, positioned so that the three indentations on its end looked like a face. That's right. People let themselves be bullied by a coconut.

A purely logical person would never let a mere image of eyes, much less of a coconut, influence behavior, but our brain is so busy processing the millions of bytes of information in our environment that many of our "decisions" happen without logic getting involved at all. You can see how at least some of what seems like a voluntary thought ("I think I'll have a candy," "I think I'll have some cereal," or "I think I'll contribute a dollar to the coffee fund") turns out to be an automatic response to your environment.

Luckily, you can use this power for good. You can turn any one of your daily routines into an opportunity to trigger positive behavior. For example, every morning as I towel off after my shower, I say a blessing over each part of my body:

I bless my feet for walking this road with me, and I bless my legs for giving me something to stand on.

I bless my hips for their sway, my belly for its curve, and my heart for its tender beat.

---

* M. Bateson, D. Nettle, and G. Roberts, "Cues of Being Watched Enhance Cooperation in a Real-World Setting," *Biology Letters* 2, no. 3 (2006): 412–14, www.ncbi.nlm.nih.gov/pmc/articles/PMC1686213.

I bless my arms for all the hugging and my hands for their good work.

I gaze at my face as I would the face of a beloved child and say thank you for all the expressions.

And I say a special blessing for any of the parts that are missing or broken or suffering from neglect.

(By the way, you can get a free downloadable PDF of this blessing, as well as the other poems featured in this book, at www.StartRightWhereYouAre.com.)

LITTLE CHANGES ACTION STEP: What's a behavior of yours that you suspect is being influenced by your environment? Make a conscious decision to change it today.

27. ⟶ New Thought versus Old Tapes

OF THE APPROXIMATELY sixty to seventy thousand thoughts we have each day, most of them are exactly the same as the thoughts we had yesterday. Not incidentally, most of these thoughts seem to be negative or critical, which is why making a deliberate move toward positivity and happiness can feel so weird. (By the way, no one really knows how many thoughts we have per day, but the nice people at LONI, the Laboratory of Neuro Imaging at the University of Southern California, have offered up seventy thousand as a nonscientific best guess.*)

So how can we cultivate new thoughts?

Here's how you can tell a new thought from the old tapes. Old tapes:

- sound like the voice of a parent, other family member or teacher.
- contain the phrase, "I always think that..." For example, "I would make a stop-action claymation movie, but I always think, 'That's been done already, so why should I bother?'" Or "I would try to sell my jewelry, but then I always think, 'That'll be too much trouble.' So I don't do it."

---

* Laboratory of Neuro Imaging, *Brain Trivia*, www.loni.usc.edu/about_loni /education/brain_trivia.php, accessed June 21, 2016.

- make you feel small, sad, limited, and shut down.
- sound like conventional wisdom. Conventional wisdom applies only to conventional people doing conventional things, and when it comes to your new thoughts, that ain't us.

In contrast, a new thought shows up like this:

- "Oh!" (I love it when I hear people make that chiming "Oh!" sound of discovery. It's plum delightful.)
- "I've never thought of that before." Or "I've never thought about it in that way before."
- "I wonder if…"
- "Maybe I could…"
- It feels expansive and intriguing.
- It offers opportunity and hope.
- It gives you the giggles, makes you cry, or provokes some other unusual reaction that you can't easily explain.

Please, oh, please, start recognizing old tapes for the unhelpful burden that they are, and start to cultivate anything that feels like a new thought.

The new thoughts you have are guiding you somewhere, so no matter how impractical or impossible they may seem, stop rejecting them out of hand. Use your intuition to tune in to your new thoughts, and then use your big, sexy brain to start testing and experimenting. Use your marvelous critical thinking skills to examine the habituated beliefs that are keeping you stuck. Use your dream-mind to tune in to the deeper "belly" wisdom that you may have been ignoring. Activate your imagination, your feelings, and your intuition, and then apply some good, old-fashioned cognition for best results.

> Conventional wisdom is for conventional people doing conventional things.

One last thing: If you happen to have people in your life who scoff at words like *intuition* or *inner wisdom*, just use the words like *hunch* or *guess* instead. As in "How did I know that today was the day to circle back around and make the sale to that big client who's already turned us down three times? Just a lucky guess, I guess!"

> Use your intuition to tune in to your new thoughts, and then use your big, sexy brain to start testing and experimenting.

LITTLE CHANGES ACTION STEP: Place your hand on your belly, take a deep breath, and ask yourself, "What does my inner wisdom want me to know right now?" You could end up with a clear desire for a grilled cheese sandwich — or perhaps an idea for a whole new direction for your life.

28. ➡ How My Intuition Led Me to Live in Paradise

SOME PEOPLE DESCRIBE THEIR INTUITION as a gut feeling, and others know it by the goose bumps they feel. Some people describe a quality of seeing — things coming into focus, or colors seeming brighter — and others describe feeling suddenly hot or cold as they hear the still, small voice within. My intuition sounds like a gong, and it feels like a swell of recognition, as though I'm finally remembering something I'd forgotten.

Sometimes it's hard for people to remember a time when their intuition or inner wisdom worked for them — after all, it can be a subterranean process — so let me tell you two stories that might spark your own memories of when you had knowledge without cognition.

> My intuition feels like a swell of recognition, as though I'm finally remembering something I'd forgotten.

When I was an undergrad at Northwestern University, I was sharing an apartment that, like so many Chicago-area apartments, consisted of a front room and then a long hallway with bedrooms leading off it that terminated in the kitchen. I walked in one winter's day and looked down the hallway toward the kitchen. There, in silhouette, seated in profile, was a woman I had never met. It turned out she was in a class with one of my roommates, and they had just become friendly, so she had come over for a study session. I didn't know anything about her, but I remember thinking, "*There* you are." I felt that gong of recognition reverberate in my belly. It was like coming home. It was like, "Look. There you are. I have been waiting for you, for my friend, and I didn't even know I was waiting for you." Her name is Margaret, and we are still as close as sisters. That feeling has happened for me only two other times, both with people who also ended up being hugely influential in my life. Perhaps you've had a similar experience?

In 1994, I had just moved to Los Angeles from Chicago, and some friends invited me to go to church with them. Being new to town, I said, "Sure. Why not?" The church turned out to be a liberal, open and affirming, we-love-everybody kind of place, and it became my church home for many years. It's such a lovey-dovey place that "hug time" (known in some churches as "greeting time" or "passing of the peace") goes on for some time, as people are so eager to chat. I, of course, didn't know anyone except my friends, and so the people around me greeted me warmly and then, understandably, went on to visit with one another. Two women near me were talking, and I overheard one say something to the other about Carpinteria.

Once again that distinctive gong reverberated in my belly, and the thought arose, "That's my spot." I didn't know what Carpinteria was, or where it was, but I knew it was for me. I mentally filed the name away. Several years later, when I finally made my first visit to Carpinteria, we drove down the main street to where it dead-ends at the beach and parked. Now, to someone who lives in LA, free, nonmetered beach parking is completely unheard-of and seems, no kidding, sort of magical. We got out of the car and walked out onto the sand. Just then, a pod of dolphins swam by, and my then-husband said, "Well, there's your welcome committee." And so it was. I felt entirely at home.

Over the years I would come up to Carpinteria for lunch whenever I needed a break, or we'd come for a long weekend, and while I loved it, it seemed impossible that I would ever be able to live there full time. Then, in early 2012, the circumstances of my life changed. Everything crumbled. My life; my marriage; even, in a way, my business…well, it all fell apart into a million pieces, the way life does sometimes. I spent six weeks on the couch crying, which is what you do when your life falls apart. Then I had one tiny, flickering thought: "Maybe…I could go to Carpinteria."

I told everyone I was going on a writing retreat. I got a short-term rental, and in just a few weeks I had completed the proposal for what would be my first non-self-published book. And I could feel my soul starting to heal. Then I got another short-term rental, and then I found a long-term rental, packed up, and moved here. It was the best decision I have ever made. I feel about this town the way some people talk about their soul mates. I'm ambivalent about the concept of soul mate for individuals, but I'm convinced it's a real thing for geographical locations. Because every time I look out the window, every day when I walk on the beach, every time I even think about the fact that I live here, I swoon.

In an interesting parallel, after we had one of the most loving and kindhearted divorces on record, my ex-husband moved to a cabin in the woods that is his dream come true. We're still friends, and we often wonder at how funny and sad it is that we had to separate from each other in order to find home.

My Carpinteria story played out over almost twenty years. I've had other intuitive moments that play out immediately. How about you? Think back on your own life. Think about a time when you really had that knowing, that deep knowing, and what it was like, and what it felt like.

Pay close enough attention, and your intuition just might lead you home.

LITTLE CHANGES ACTION STEP: When has obeying your still, small voice paid off for you? Work that story into conversation today.

29. ➟ Ten Ways to Cultivate Your Intuition

WE DON'T GET MUCH EDUCATION in developing or trusting our intuition, and like a muscle, it gets stronger with practice, so here are ten fun, easy ways to cultivate your intuition.

1. Break your routine. Do something different. Anything. Drive a different way to work, walk on the other side of the street, create an all-new sandwich. This will help you stay alert and in the moment, so you can notice when your intuition is pulling at your sleeve.

2. At a restaurant, choose to order the very first thing that you see on the menu. If nothing else, it's pleasant to have more time for conversation and less time for silently obsessing about the calorie difference between the tuna salad and the Cobb.

3. Take the long way home. Just let the car take you wherever it wants to go. Or walk a different way home. Deliberately get lost. See where you end up.

4. Keep some kind of notebook beside your bed and record just the images from your dreams. I never worry about remembering the plot — dream logic is too confusing to try to capture — but I usually remember a few images, and those can be quite illuminating.

5. Try some version of automatic writing. If you like the idea of friendly spirits or guides writing through you, go for it. If not, just try to write faster than your mind can think.

6. *Right hand–left hand exercise.* Let your dominant hand ask a question that you really want the answer to, and let your nondominant hand write the answer. (Yes, the writing of your nondominant hand will look like that of a deranged kindergartner. No worries.) Keep the dialogue going until you feel satisfied.

7. *Talk to animals.* Get quiet and communicate in thought pictures with the animals in your life.

8. *Connect with new people in your daily life.* If you feel a pull toward someone you don't know, reach out in some way. Make eye contact with people at the grocery store and at the gas station. Allow yourself to notice what you believe at first glance about them. (In other words, when you really look at someone, you might get little flickers of thought: "She looks lonely," or "I bet he was wild as a teenager." Just let that impression bubble up.)

9. *Truthfully answer the question, "How are you?"* On being asked, take a second to check in with yourself and give a real answer. Caution: this might lead to a real conversation.

10. *Obey the "How dumb would I feel?" rule.* This rule kicks in when I pull into a parking space with my tote holding my computer on the front seat and think, "Oh, I don't have to put that in the trunk; I'm sure it will be fine." Then I think, "Yup, I'm sure it will be fine, but how dumb would I feel if I came back out here and it was gone?" I would feel pretty darn dumb, especially since I had just had this conversation with myself. Make it a daily practice to pay attention to your niggling thoughts and suspicions.

LITTLE CHANGES ACTION STEP: Choose one intuition cultivator from the list above and do it today.

30. → The Intuition Killers

JUST AS YOU CAN DEVELOP your inner wisdom, there are also some easy ways to suppress it. Here are six killers of intuition:

1. The need to be right. The need to be smart, documented, and logical in all of your decisions will cause you to ignore the whispers of your soul and do foolish things, like marrying someone who "looks good on paper" or taking a job just for the money.

2. The safety of "I don't know." Sometimes when you say, "I don't know," it's because actually you *do* know, and you just don't like it. Other times you allow yourself to stay confuddled so that you don't have to commit to a decision. If this is a habit of yours, try using the life coach's trick of saying, "If I did know the answer, it might be..."

3. Fatigue and dehydration. As we've discussed, physical depletion often leads directly to poor brain function and unreliable interpretations of the signals your inner wisdom is trying to send you.

4. Depression. When you are caught up in hopelessness, grief, and nonstop self-criticism, it is very hard for you to hear that deep, calm, knowing voice within, and even harder to trust it.

5. Talking yourself into and out of decisions. When you second-guess yourself, you confuse yourself and develop self-mistrust.

6. Routine. Being on autopilot causes you to stagnate and go to sleep.

LITTLE CHANGES ACTION STEP: List two more intuition killers. Now list four possible antidotes to torpor. Here are some of my antidotes: play the music of the Talking Heads, Elvis Costello, or Buddy Holly; read a story out loud, preferably to a child; run or walk as fast as I can for one block; throw stones into the ocean; nap; call a smart friend to meet me for an impromptu cocktail; draw a tiny circle on a piece of paper, and then draw a very big circle around the tiny one, reminding me that the tiny circle represents what I think I know, and the big circle is everything I don't know.

31. ➤ Values-Based Decision Making

SOMETIMES WHEN YOU ARE TRYING to make a decision, you hop back and forth, giving everything equal weight inside your mind. And the reasons for and reasons against just swirl around, making you feel more confused than, perhaps, you actually are. The fact is that not everything has equal importance to you.

So, when trying to decide whether to go to Hawaii on vacation, you might start spinning a lazy Susan of thoughts, "It's a long flight...and it's an expensive plane ticket...but it's so romantic....I'd love to swim with wild dolphins...and surfing could be fun...but I'm not sure where we'd stay...and it's a long flight..." See what I mean about the lazy Susan spin?

The following exercise is a delightful way to blend your inner wisdom, personal preferences, and pure logic. You can find a video of me walking you through this exercise at www.StartRight WhereYouAre.com, and here are the steps:

1. State the decision to be made. Make it a statement, not a question.
2. Write out the pros and cons.
3. Assign each item a number between one and ten, based on its importance to you.

So while "long flight" is a valid consideration, when you reflect more deeply, you realize that you don't actually mind plane travel, so that might only rate a 3, while "swim with wild dolphins" might thrill you to bits, so you give it a 10. Notice that this process is meant to be deliberately subjective. Your spouse, who hates to fly and doesn't like to swim, may take a look at the same list and give "long flight" an 8 and the dolphins a 2. The numbers alone may make your decision for you, or you may want to do some additional investigation into your thoughts, feelings, and assumptions. Note that we're only considering what's important to *you*, *right now*, in *this particular* instance.

If you like, you can list the same number of pros and cons, and then total up the numbers and see which side wins.

I once did this exercise with a client named Taylor who was working at a successful advertising firm but was seriously considering quitting to start her own interior design business. Now, in my experience, by the time a person is asking out loud a question like "Should I quit my job?" or "Should I leave my relationship?" the ship has already sailed. Usually, by that time, the person has actually already amassed all the evidence they need, and they're just looking for permission to act on the decision. Not always, but often. Has that happened to you?

> In my experience, by the time a person is asking out loud a question like "Should I quit my job?" or "Should I leave my relationship?" the ship has already sailed.

I reminded Taylor that we wanted to list the issues at hand as though it were a debate. So her statement was "I should keep the job I have." Her pro column was "Reasons in Favor of Keeping the Job I Have," and the con column was "Reasons against Keeping the Job I Have."

Taylor's original list looked like this:

I SHOULD KEEP THE JOB I HAVE
PRO/Reasons in Favor of Keeping the Job I Have
    It is the devil I know
    I am good at it, so I feel confident

I could get a promotion (maybe — won't know for three
 months)
I like most of my coworkers
Staying feels easier than looking for a new gig

CON / Reasons against Keeping the Job I Have
I am bored out of my mind
My boss is rude, angry, and unsupportive
I really have a bigger dream of doing something else
The commute is too long
I don't feel like what we do really matters — it doesn't make
 a contribution to the planet

In the next step, Taylor went down the two columns and,
after a quick gut check, rated each item on a scale of one to ten to
indicate how important it was to her.

PRO / Reasons in Favor of Keeping the Job I Have
It is the devil I know — 3
I am good at it, so I feel confident — 5
I could get a promotion (maybe — won't know for three
 months) — 7
I like most of my coworkers — 9
Staying feels easier than looking for a new gig — 3

CON / Reasons against Keeping the Job I Have
I am bored out of my mind — 10
My boss is rude, angry, and unsupportive — 4
I really have a bigger dream of doing something else — 10
The commute is too long — 5
I don't feel like what we do really matters — it doesn't make
 a contribution to the planet — 3

Then Taylor simply added up the scores. The reasons for keeping her job scored 27 points, and a large part of that number was attributable to how much she liked her coworkers. Reasons against keeping it scored 32. She handed in her notice fourteen days later. She also created a standing monthly lunch date with her officemates so that they wouldn't lose touch, and that group has turned out to be an indispensable resource and support group for all of them.

These numbers may or may not be the final decision maker for you, but this process is an easy way to start letting your values guide your choices so that you are living a life that is in concert with your values. When your behavior is consistent with what you say is important to you, we call it integrity.

I find this strategy especially helpful when money is part of the decision. It's easy to let money get out of proportion to the other considerations. You may think to yourself "Oh, this trip to my nephew's graduation is expensive. It would cost me five hundred dollars." But when you examine the five hundred dollars in relationship to all the benefits, like supporting your nephew, making memories with your family, and eating some delicious hometown food, you may find that the money is not that big a deal. And that's okay. If something is not that big a deal to you, let it not be that big a deal. It is you who has to live with the choice. You don't need to concern yourself with what anybody else would do. If some busybody does question your decision, you can always say, "I weighed all my options carefully, and I also listened to my heart." Only a real Scrooge can argue with that. You are allowed to navigate your life based on what truly matters to you.

LITTLE CHANGES ACTION STEP: Try this activity right now on some real or theoretical question, just as an experiment.

32. ⟶ Happy Grown-Up Naked Time

As NEAR AS I CAN TELL, no one over the age of forty-three, whether they are in a committed relationship or not, is having any sex at all. And if they are, it's the same, boring routine, punctuated by the occasional lift from new lingerie. I hope you are an exception to this, but if not, I might have a solution for you.

A 2015 study of more than thirty thousand Americans conducted over four decades suggests that the happiest couples have sex once a week.* The study goes on to say that it isn't clear if people who are happier have sex once a week, or if having sex once a week makes people happier. Either way, it's a win-win.

Because I know that there are lots of people who can't or prefer not to have sex, and lots of people who don't have a partner, I would like to suggest that we replace weekly sex with weekly Happy Grown-Up Naked Time.

With or without a partner, Happy Grown-Up Naked Time is meant to be a stress-free exploration of the body. It is a time to get reacquainted with your own skin. It is a time to experience the sheer pleasure of the physical self. You can use this time for foot

---

* Amy Muise, Ulrich Schimmack, and Emily A. Impett, "Sexual Frequency Predicts Greater Well-Being, but More Is Not Always Better," *Social Psychological and Personality Science* 7 (May 2016): 295–302, spp.sagepub.com/content /7/4/295.abstract.

rubs, for stretching, for finding new spots that are ticklish. I think it's especially nice to caress skin in half-time or quarter-time. That is, take the normal pace at which you might stroke skin, and go twice as slowly. Now go twice as slowly as that. Humming sounds are optional.

Science backs up the obvious pleasure of slow touch. In a 2013 study, researchers in the United Kingdom discovered that slow caresses can improve the brain's ability to create and sustain a healthy sense of self.*

Happy Grown-Up Naked Time can be used by couples to cuddle, to talk, to trade massages, to make out, to spoon, to masturbate themselves or each other, and even, should the mood strike, have sex. But there should be no pressure or expectation to have sex or to achieve orgasm. This is time for intimacy, acceptance, and exploration. It is meant to be cheerful, calm, and stimulating. It is not necessarily erotic. This is a time for adults to be adults together. I remember when my friend Annie was the full-time caregiver for her toddler, she said that by the end of the day, she felt covered in sticky fingerprints. "I didn't even feel like my body belonged to me," she recalls, "and I certainly didn't feel sexy or like having sex." Happy Grown-Up Naked Time provides a reset button for stressed-out parents like Annie and allows them time to reclaim their adult bodies and adult passion.

> This is a time for adults to be adults together.

I had the good fortune to do a joint teleclass with a dear friend of mine, the wonderful sexual empowerment expert Amy Jo Goddard, author of *Woman on Fire: 9 Elements to Wake Up*

---

* L. Crucianelli, N. K. Metcalf, A. Fotopoulou, and P. M. Jenkinson, "Bodily Pleasure Matters: Velocity of Touch Modulates Body Ownership during the Rubber Hand Illusion," *Frontiers in Psychology* 4 (October 2013), dx.doi.org/10.3389/fpsyg.2013.00703.

Your Erotic Energy, Personal Power, and Sexual Intelligence, about the relationship between creative energy and sexual energy. In answering a call-in question about where to begin reigniting your mojo when you're feeling all dried up, Amy Jo recommended the following practice:

Take a deep, cleansing breath, and rest your hands gently on the top of your head. Slowly run your hands from the crown of your head down over your ears and neck and shoulders. Return your hands to the top of your head and bring them down across your face. Allow your hands to travel slowly down your arms, then your torso, your legs, and feet.

Amy Jo actually talked everyone through this brief exercise during the call, and the people who were there were surprised and delighted by the immediate positive effect. It's lovely to know that something so simple — just acknowledging your body with your own hands — can lead to an increased sense of well-being and pleasure. You can find the free audio of this illuminating interview at www.StartRightWhereYouAre.com.

Happy Grown-Up Naked Time can happen in water — hot tubs are particularly nice — or out of doors. It can happen in hotel rooms, if that fits your style and your budget. If I were making the rules, I would say no TV or videos, because I think this is about human-to-human contact, but do what works for you. Dim lighting takes some of the pressure off, and candlelight makes any room feel special, but full light is better for more, ahem, scientific observations. When in doubt, choose comfort.

If you're worried because you don't know what to say to suggest such a thing, try something like this: "Sweetheart, I love you, and I want to make sure that we stay connected with one another. I was thinking about scheduling a weekly 'Happy Grown-Up Naked Time' date on Wednesday nights in which we could just lie around nude for a half-hour or so and see what happens. What do you think about that?" Once you're actually naked, you might say something like, "I feel a little shy and silly right now, but I want to be braver in my communications, so is it okay if I ask you to run your fingertips very lightly across my back?" Suggest whatever seems nice. Perhaps you could invent a game in which each person has to make three requests and give three compliments. Experiment. Don't fall into a rut.

Use the following words to inspire new activities whether you are playing alone or with a partner: drumming, counting, I'm-Not-Touching-You, fingertips, drawing, paintbrush, leather, Push-Me-Pull-You, balancing act, unusual accents, and the always useful, "Yes, and..." Make your own list. Challenge yourself to try new things.

Happy Grown-Up Naked Time often leads to Happy Grown-Up Nap Time, which I'm 100 percent in favor of. I believe the world would be an infinitely better place if we all took more frequent naps.

Little Changes Action Step: Close your eyes, and gently run your hands down and across your head, face, neck, and shoulders. Repeat as desired.

33. ➡ There's No More-Perfect You

YOU CANNOT SCREW UP YOUR LIFE. Your life is un-screw-up-able. You cannot do your life wrong. There is no such thing as a wrong choice, or a missed opportunity, or something you should have done differently. Even the decisions you've made that you regret, or the ones that have led to an unfortunate outcome, were not wrong.

I realize this can sound radical, but it's true.

It seems as if there are better decisions and worse ones, but there aren't. There are only the decisions you make. You are the only one leading your life, and you are only doing it once. There is no alternative. There can be no "better" or "worse" when there's only one.

> You cannot screw up your life.

See, if there was another, more perfect version of you who made different decisions, and that person was healthier, more prosperous, or more successful than you are, then we could say that you had screwed up. But there isn't. There is only you, making the best decisions you can with the information you have at the time. Just like everybody else.

So what happens inside your mind when you realize that every decision you've made was the right one? And that everything that has ever happened to you must be the right thing to have happened, because it is the only thing that happened?

Well-intentioned people often try to comfort others by saying, "Everything happens for a reason," but I'm not sure if that's true. I do know that everything that happens, happens. And that we can decide what the reason is. We are the meaning makers of our own lives. We get to tell the story however we want.

So you can tell the story of your life as though you have been wronged, or as though everything has conspired for the greater good. You can tell the story of your life as though you have been victimized, or you can accept full responsibility for your reactions and results. You are someone who's been getting a PhD in being you. You're still learning, and there are wise teachers who will tell you that learning is why we are here. We are here for our soul's education.

"Even the horrible things?" I can hear you wondering. "How can I possibly say that losing my loved one was right? Or that my brother's debilitating, long-term illness is good?" I'm not saying those things are right or good, I'm saying they happened. And you have the ability to choose how you think about them. Nature is indifferent to our cries, and heartbreak happens to everyone.

We all suffer. Everyone gets the same amount of pain. Everyone's life is as hard for them as your life is for you. Some people's stories are more dramatic, or seem, from the outside, to be easier or harder, but pain is pain, and we all get equal rations.

Luckily, we also all get the same capacity for joy. Not everybody takes advantage of that, of course, but still — the joy is always there, just waiting for you.

LITTLE CHANGES ACTION STEP: You may have been running a story in your head about how you made a bad decision in the past, or how you wish a decision had worked out better. Write yourself a 5-Minute Poem about that loss or disappointment, and see if you can find the blessing in it.

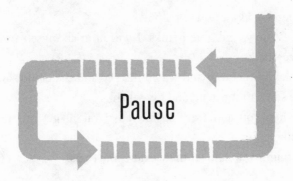

Pause

The Desert

Dear God,

I honestly thought I knew what I was doing.

Clearly, I've been mistaken.

I was so confident that what I was doing was right...I mean, everyone else seemed to believe it was right, too. They all nodded and smiled encouragingly. Or maybe I just thought they did.

But my willful path has led me straight into the desert.

So here I am...hot and bothered. Lost.

I can't even tell which direction is which.

Even my path to here has been erased by shifting sands.

So.

Here we are.

Without all that success and approval that I was so desperate for, I can feel only you.

I can only sit quietly and feel your loving presence amid my frustrations and failures and crushing disappointment.

I imagine you whispering to me, reminding me of the truth of who I am: your favorite child, the Beloved of God.

And I sigh into myself.

Just a person, alone and not alone.

I will rest now, and give thanks. I will nourish myself now, and give thanks.

I will play in the sand and watch the sky and the clouds and feel the sun and the wind and give thanks.

And, when you and I are so moved, I might get up and start walking.

Or we might wait and let the world come to us.

We'll see.

Love,
Me

34. ⟶ Nothing Bad Is Happening

YOU KNOW HOW WHEN TRAFFIC IS HORRIBLE and you got a late start to begin with and then someone honks at you for completely no reason and you start to get a bit...short-tempered?

Or when you're squished into your airline seat (since I'm almost six feet tall, I'm always squished) and there's a loud talker seated next to you and you've just realized that you left your novel at home so you're facing a five-hour flight and you've got absolutely nothing to read or watch...can you feel the stress clench up your shoulders?

When my inner calm deserts me and my sense of humor is nowhere to be found and I can practically feel the cortisol flooding my system, there is one sentence that works for me.

"Nothing bad is happening."

And then I try to exhale.

"Nothing bad is happening."

This handy little phrase snaps everything back into perspective.

After all, the circumstances may be uncomfortable, or even unpleasant, but that doesn't mean that things are bad.

In fact, maybe it's an opportunity for me to open my eyes and notice the people around me — maybe make a joke with the flight attendant, or, in gridlock, smile at the driver stuck in the lane next to me.

Maybe it's an opportunity to turn off the yelling voice inside my head that wants to insist, "It's not supposed to be like this!" and tune in to the gentle voice that says, "Everything is unfolding — watch and see."

Nothing bad is happening.

I've held that thought through divorce, through surgery, through severe financial setbacks, and guess what. It's always been true.

Please don't misunderstand me: I'm not saying that you should ignore feelings of anger, danger, disappointment, or sadness. Those feelings are powerful indicators that something is amiss, and they need safe expression and examination.

(And you know I think that the best thing to do with strong feelings is to turn them into some 5-Minute Art. A quick drawing of what "nothing ever works out for me" looks like can work wonders at transforming that painful thought.)

I'll tell you a story that might help make this clear. Some years ago, I got a call from my doctor's office that there was something they didn't like about the results of my recent mammogram, and they wanted me to come in for another exam. "Sure," I said. And inside I thought, "I'll go in, but nothing bad is happening." So I got to the appointment and endured the second mammogram (if you've never had one, just imagine a big, cold machine giving you a big, cold titty-twister — it is so very not fun), and then the technician got a concerned look on her face. "Wait right here," she said. "Fine," I thought, "but nothing bad is happening." So I waited, and then waited some more in a different room, because they had decided I needed an ultrasound.

It was during the ultrasound that I had the unnervingly flippant thought, "Even if there is some kind of problem, it's still not anything bad. We'll get a diagnosis and deal with it. That's what life is: dealing with things. Or maybe I'll die, in which case I won't have to deal with it after all." I was a little shocked to find myself so calm. After a few more worried looks and long stretches hanging out in a bare exam room, they finally told me that the radiologist wanted to see me.

Another wait in a hallway, and finally the harried-looking radiologist poked his head out of his office, pointed at me and said, "Bennett?" I nodded. "You're fine. You can go."

I was right: nothing bad was happening.

Now, I know some people who would have started worrying right away, and who would have spent the two weeks before the appointment twisting themselves into knots over imagined outcomes. And I know people who would have allowed their equilibrium to be disturbed by the long afternoon at the clinic. I was tremendously pleased with myself that I stayed unruffled. (It was a real personal growth milestone, one of those moments of realizing, "Hey! This self-help stuff really works!")

Another time I had invested quite a bit of money to partner with a friend on a project. We were both excited about the growth and possibilities. Imagine how disappointed I was when this friend failed to hold up her end of the bargain. My lower self wanted to throw a tantrum about how I'd been taken advantage of and ripped off. But my higher self said, "Nothing bad is happening."

I paused to examine my own behavior in the partnership: I hadn't insisted on a clear agreement, and I had ignored several warning signs that her commitment to the project was faltering. I was as responsible as she was, and I began to consider the money not lost but rather an investment in my ongoing education. A year or two later, that same friend made an introduction that created an opportunity in which I was able to earn nearly five times the amount I had "lost" on our project. I was so glad that I hadn't burned my bridges with her and that I was willing to face some uncomfortable truths about myself in order to become a better business owner.

LITTLE CHANGES ACTION STEP: The everyday annoyances, the little temper tantrums, the self-righteousness, martyrdom, and prickliness — those are signs to tell yourself, "Nothing bad is happening." And see if you can figure out, when things aren't unfolding in the way you would choose, how they might still be unfolding perfectly.

35. ➤ Your Slightly Future Self

IMAGINE A SLIGHTLY MORE SUCCESSFUL VERSION of you living in the not very distant future. Notice how that person behaves, what they're wearing, what mood that person is in. The next time you're not sure what to do, ask yourself, "How would my slightly future self solve this problem?" This easy strategy is a great way to lose weight, make more money, jettison unfortunate habits, and get in the fast lane — or the slow lane, if that's more your jam.

There's one more tool to help you with this: go ahead and relax back into yourself the way we did in our earlier meditations. Feel your center, that heartwood, that core. Take a breath. Inhale — two, three, four. Hold — two, three, four, five, six, seven. Exhale — two, three, four, five, six, seven, eight. Allow a vision of your slightly future self to appear in your mind. You may just get a glimpse. Notice I said your "slightly" future self, so this is you sometime in the next year or two. Have it be a very joyful version of yourself, a very successful version of you. It's not that everything is radically different, but this is a future in which things are better for you.

> How would my slightly future self solve this problem?

See if you can't create a little slideshow, or a little film in your mind of your slightly future self. As it plays, notice if you are slightly happier, slightly more engaged, slightly more creative, slightly more prosperous — and answer the questions below:

123

1. What does your slightly future self look like?
2. What is the expression on their face?
3. What is your slightly future self wearing?
4. How are they behaving?
5. How are they interacting with the world?
6. How does that person start their day?
7. What do they do first thing?
8. How is their life the same as yours right now?
9. How is it different?
10. Does your slightly future self have a theme song?

From now on, when you need to make a decision, you can ask yourself, "What would my slightly future self do right now? How would that person handle this situation? How would that person dress for today? How would that person speak up? What does that person eat? What does that person stress out about or not stress out about? Where is that person's focus?"

That is how you can bring deep and lasting change to your life: when you let that slightly better, slightly future self make decisions in the now for you. Little change, big difference.

LITTLE CHANGES ACTION STEP: What does your slightly future self want you to do today? Or even right this second?

36. ➡ You're Ready Now

IT MAKES ME SAD when I hear people decline an opportunity because they claim that they are "not ready."

Now, perhaps they are just finding what they think of as a nice, inoffensive way to say no. And no is a terrific answer. A nice, clean, empowered no can be almost better than a yes, as it indicates that you have the courage of your decisions, and that you're willing to take the consequences.

No, I don't want to expand my business right now.

No, I don't want to take that workshop.

No, I don't want to perform my piece, or enter it in the art show, or make my work public.

No, I don't want to apply for that promotion.

If your no sounds clear and strong when you say it out loud, and you feel good about the decision, then hooray. More power to you. The famous billionaire Warren Buffett has been quoted as saying, "The difference between successful people and really successful people is that really successful people say no to almost everything." I've been working on saying no to more things myself, so that I can give myself more fully to the things I say yes to. No is a noble practice.

What concerns me is the "Yes, but" habit — someone who says they want to do something, and then, in the same breath, denies themselves the opportunity to do it. "I'd love to learn to tango, but I could never take a class like that." It's like watching a hungry person reach for a plate of food, and then snatch their own hand back, imagining that maybe their hunger will just go away, or that there will be a better time to eat later on.

Your desire is your hunger. And just as hunger alerts you to eat so that you stay alive, your desire alerts you to the next step toward your best life. Desire is how you know where to go. Desire is your engraved invitation to your own party. Desire is the flame — the sacred energy — that will give you the courage to move forward.

Does this sound like I'm giving you permission to become a great, wallowing id, governed by nothing but the selfish thought, "I *want*"? Well, I kind of am. Because in my experience, many of the people who read these kinds of books — that's you, by the way — have been putting others first for so long that you have almost forgotten how to pose the question, "What do I want?" Every decision gets complicated by a chorus of voices in your head, wondering what other people will think, and what the repercussions of one choice or another will be, and whether it is really acceptable for you to do this thing or that. And your own still, small voice gets drowned out. This is how you end up in a life that is, at best, kind of boring and, at worst, soul destroying.

> Desire is your engraved invitation to your own party.

The top three excuses I hear when people want something but are unwilling to commit are:

1. I don't have the money.
2. I don't have the time.
3. I'm not ready.

I notice that most people find the time and the money for whatever's important to them. You've probably noticed how the same people who always claim to be broke are often the same ones who are first in line to purchase the latest high-priced electronic gadget. And the same people who don't have time to do anything can be found driving three hours each way on a school night to hear their favorite band in concert. Now, I'm all in favor of new gadgets and seeing a favorite band, but how did they find that money? How did they find the time? They found it because the desire to have or do the thing outweighed any other consideration. You've had that experience yourself: you get very clear that you want to do something, or go somewhere, or buy something, and suddenly the ways and means to do that exact thing show up. It feels like magic. And while magic may have something to do with it, I think it has more to do with how desire sharpens your mind.

One of the things your brain is best at is finding what it's looking for. If I tell you to find all the things that are smaller than a bread box wherever you are right now, you will automatically start doing that. In fact, you might even keep doing it later on today. (You also might wonder what a bread box is: it's a box you keep bread in. You're welcome.) This is why affirmations can be helpful; when you repeat a phrase like "I am a lucky person" or "I am loving and loved," your brain will seek and find evidence to support that thought. When you think a thought like "I want to go to Paris but I could never afford it," your brain will keep finding evidence that you want to go to Paris and can't afford it.

So start paying attention to your desire. Ask yourself several times a day, "What do I want right now?" And if that question is hard for you, try asking, "How can I make this moment more *me* right now?" See if you can't give yourself what you want.

This brings me back around to the readiness issue. If you are noticing an opportunity, it's probably because your desire is nudging

> How can I make this moment more *me* right now?

you to notice it. Which means that you are at least ready to investigate the options.

Now you may be thinking, "Okay, I'm willing to admit that I want X, Y, or Z, but I have no idea how to get it." Honey, of course you don't know how. You've never done it before. How could you possibly know how? Figuring out the how is the fun part.

You may have been led to believe that a smart person figures everything out in advance. But life doesn't work that way. Creativity doesn't work that way. Love, parenthood, writing, riding BMX bikes — for all of the most interesting things in life, you start out with no idea how you are supposed to do such a thing. But if you stay curious and open, lo and behold! The way will be made clear.

But the way is only made clear after you make your decision. I wish it could be the other way around, but it's not. When you commit to a decision, then and only then is the path revealed. If you allow fear and confusion and second-guessing to swirl up and obscure your desire, how to get there will remain a mystery to you forever. Either way, you have a self-perpetuating cycle. Either your desire leads you to commitment, which leads you to the how and the way, or it leads you to self-doubt, which closes off the how or the way.

> When you commit to a decision, then and only then is the path revealed.

LITTLE CHANGES ACTION STEP: Can you think of a time when you wanted something implausible but committed to it anyway, and then found a way to make it happen? Could you try that again today?

37. → Set Good, Better, Best Goals

IF YOU ARE A FRUSTRATED OVERACHIEVER, you might be causing yourself pain because you think that nothing you do is ever quite good enough. Even the accomplishments that you know are admirable somehow get diminished. You graduated from law school, but you weren't first in your class. You got the promotion, but it would have been better if you'd gotten it six months ago. You sold five thousand dollars' worth of products, but now you wish it had been ten thousand. If you get into the habit of creating good, better, and best goals, you can stop constantly moving the finish line on yourself.

Let's say you are offering a workshop. You might set the "good" goal at signing up the minimum number of people you need to feel like it's worth it — let's say seven. The "better" number you might set at ten. And the "best" number, your "drinks are on me" goal, might be fourteen. This approach allows you to be both realistic and ambitious. It permits you to take remedial action if enrollment is below seven and to truly congratulate yourself on any number over ten, rather than getting nine people in the workshop and then wallowing in disappointment because you secretly wanted fourteen.

You can also use this approach for deadlines. It would be good to have this done by Friday, it would be better to have it

> Stop moving the finish line.

done by Wednesday, but it would be best if it were done by Tuesday morning.

Finally, you can also use this system for "feeling" goals — goals that are more a state of being than a metric. If you wanted to feel more forgiving toward someone you felt had hurt you, you might set a "good" goal such as "I will stop telling the story of how I got hurt to myself and others," a "better" goal of "I can think about that person and stay peaceful in my heart, but I don't want to see them," and a "best" goal of "I could see this person and be genuinely glad, because they taught me so much."

LITTLE CHANGES ACTION STEP: Try this strategy out right now by completing the following sentences:

My project is:

My "good" goal is:

My "better" goal is:

My "best" goal is:

38. ➞ The Inevitable Backlash

WELL DONE, YOU. You're putting yourself in the middle of your own life, you're listening to your intuition, you're feeling supported by the Net, and suddenly...backlash.

I'm not exactly sure why this happens, but I see it all the time. No sooner does a person start making strides toward a new, better life then something comes along to derail them.

Sometimes it's a disparaging comment from a relative or friend (it's astonishing how those little zingers can stop you right in your tracks, isn't it?), and sometimes it's your own self-doubt. Sometimes there's a crisis — one of the kids gets in trouble, or the roof falls in, or the dog's legs fall off. Whatever the event, you suddenly find yourself with a perfectly good reason to quit.

Don't.

Your troubles may be happening in real life or only inside your head, but, either way, this is your big chance to handle things differently. This is your big chance to not let other people's opinions sway you. This is your big chance to not let other people's problems trample your own agenda. This is your big chance to be responsive to the situation without losing your own voice entirely.

> This crisis is your big chance to handle things differently.

So, first of all, make some 5-Minute Art about what's happening. Your feelings of guilt, obligation, resentment, anger, and fear deserve to be voiced. Once you've cleared away the clouds of feelings, you may be able to see an opportunity in what originally appeared to be a setback.

It may be that the roof falling in gives you the perfect excuse to get rid of all that junk that's cluttering up the spare room. Or perhaps the person you meet at the dog-leg repair shop is the new partner or friend you've been seeking, and the two of you end up cofounding a Society to End the Falling Off of Dogs' Legs, and a bunch of celebrities get involved, and you get to party in Malibu with the beautiful people. Stay the course. Modifications to your grand plan are inevitable, but don't abandon it.

The past four summers, I've hosted a big three-day event in Southern California called The Big Yes: How to Overcome Procrastination, Perfectionism, and Self-Doubt and Make $10,000 (or More!) from Your Creativity. It's a lot of fun, and we help creative people make great progress on their ability to profit from their work in a very short time.

Last year, the night before the event started, I got an email from a young woman I'll call Jane, who was writing to let me know that she had been so looking forward to attending The Big Yes, but she had been called into work and wouldn't be able to come after all. She expressed how disappointed she was, and I could feel the push-pull she was experiencing.

I wrote her back saying, "I can't want this for you more than you want it for yourself, but I would really urge you to make a different decision here. Because you already made an important gesture indicating your commitment to a different life — a more creatively fulfilled life — by buying a ticket to this event, and by setting aside the time to be here. I know you want to be a good employee, but now is not the time to let someone else's problem interrupt your journey."

I went on to tell her that I had spent way too much of my

young adulthood sacrificing things that were important to me on the altar of what I thought was important to my employers. And guess how those employers repaid me. They didn't. I mean, they were perfectly nice and said thank you and stuff, but I don't think they were any nicer to me than they might otherwise have been. I got the same hourly wage as always. Nobody cared that I had given up my writing time to stay late. Nobody cared that I left Thanksgiving dinner early to cover a shift. My loyalty got me almost nothing. That is loyalty to the point of self-abuse. And it was my own fault, because when they asked me for extra effort, I always said yes. I wanted to be good. I wanted to be approved of. I didn't want to be any trouble. I was hiding. I was avoiding my real life with the self-righteous excuse that they needed me at work.

They didn't need me at work that much. And they probably don't need you at work that much, either. And you know this, because you have bailed on work when there was a real, unavoidable reason for you to not be there, and you have also picked up the slack when someone else didn't show. It's not ideal, but the other people at work can figure it out. You are allowed to put yourself first every once in a while, particularly when you are busy turning yourself into someone who is ultimately going to be a better, more vibrant employee.

Sometimes the derailment doesn't come as a personal disaster or as a work emergency. Sometimes it shows up disguised as an "opportunity." You know — when your former boss calls and offers you your old job back at a little bit more money. Or when your old lover calls, just to see if you might want to get together for old times' sake.

I like to think that this is the universe having a yard sale on all your old stuff. It's as though there was a storage locker somewhere, filled with things that match your old patterns, and the minute you change your patterns, the universe decides to offer you all your old stuff one more time, just to make sure you really don't want it. Believe me, you really don't. That opportunity to leap back into the old gig or the old bed is a test of your commitment to your new pattern. So be brave, say, "No, but thank you so much for thinking of me," and move on.

I promise you that once you get a few steps down your new road, you won't even remember why you ever wanted that old stuff, because the new stuff is so sweet.

LITTLE CHANGES ACTION STEP: I never heard from Jane again. What do you imagine has happened to her since then? Make a piece of 5-Minute Art (an abstract drawing? a song? a dance? a portrait in chalk on the sidewalk?) that tells the end of Jane's story.

39. ➡ The Inevitable Backlash,
Part 2: The Inside Job

SOMETIMES THE INEVITABLE BACKLASH comes not from a crisis or from your family, coworkers, or community. Sometimes it comes from inside your own mind.

Quickly — right now — can you think of some of the ways in which you have stopped yourself from moving forward in the past? What thought made you stop?

Some people describe the thoughts that stop you as self-sabotage, or as the subconscious working against you, but I'm not certain that we have an inner destructive impulse. I think it's just that part of our mind is naturally conservative and wants to keep us safe. So, like an overprotective fussbudget trying to control a hyperactive child, no sooner do you get a creative impulse or make a strong decision than your worrying mind starts thinking of all the ways your plan could go horribly, horribly wrong.

The job of the self is to referee. It's to be the good parent, who channels the energy of the child in positive directions and soothes (or distracts) the fussbudget. You — the self — are in charge of watching your own thoughts and noticing the ones that simply aren't true or are highly unlikely, like "Everyone might hate me" or "No one will want what I have to offer," and bringing them out into the warm light of your own good judgment.

I find that saying your fears out loud helps dispel them. A fear that is very real and threatening echoing inside your head often sounds kind of silly when you say it out loud. Writing the terrifying thoughts down on paper helps, too. No sooner do you see the sentence "I might fail completely" written on a page than you think, "Well, probably not. Not *completely*, anyway."

The reason this backlash of fear and self-doubt is inevitable is that everyone experiences it. Everyone. Every famous person, every successful person, every beginner, every award-winner, every everyone. The people who dare to do what you want to do aren't any less afraid than you are (although they might be afraid of different things). Of course they're afraid. It's just that they don't let those fears stop them. If you need to, write yourself a little note that says, "Everyone is exactly as afraid as I am."

> A fear that is very real and threatening echoing inside your head often sounds kind of silly when you say it out loud.

So while the inevitable backlash is happening, stay in touch with your most evolved self. Stay calm. Stay centered. Say to yourself, "Ah, of course. These are the insecurities and worries that Sam said would come up. Look at all the monsters crawling out from every corner. Hello, monsters. You're all looking well. Nice to see you. I must be up to something really exciting if every monster I have is getting activated. How cool."

Don't engage with the monsters. Don't let them pull you down. Don't cave. Stay connected to the Net. Just keep repeating to yourself, "Nothing is more important than my well-being. I'm ready now. I'm ready now. Show me what the next step is. Guide me. I'm open. If I succeed, I promise to do the best I can with it."

You're up to it. I know you are. I know you can do it. And the world needs your good work.

LITTLE CHANGES ACTION STEP: Draw the monsters.

40. → What Are You Afraid Might Happen?

GOING BACK TO THE IDEA of writing out your thoughts so that you can see them in the full light of your best judgment (and not just in the shadowy confines of your anxiety), grab a pen and, without pondering, answer the questions and fill in the blanks below. If any of the questions seem to not apply to you or to your circumstance, feel free to modify them. See if you can surprise yourself with your own answers.

1. Write down the name of one person that you would really *like* to say no to — even if you feel certain that it's not really possible to tell them no.

2. What are you worried the result of saying no to that person would be? Fill in the blank: If I said no to _____, I might seem _____.

3. What's one element of your environment that you would like to change?

4. Fill in the blank: Changing my environment might mean _____.

5. What is one attractive diversion that distracts you from your true goals?

6. Fill in the blank: I like my attractive diversion because _____.

7. What is one thing you're afraid might happen if you were more fully committed to your goals and priorities?

8. Fill in the blank: Allowing myself to commit to my goals and priorities might make me _____.

LITTLE CHANGES ACTION STEP: Make some 5-Minute Art about what it means to be committed to your dreams, or maybe a little song. I just improvised the first part of an old-fashioned Broadway musical–style song that goes something like:

> I've got a dream
> Can't get distracted
> I've got a dream
> Do it now
> I've got a dream
> 'Bout time I acted
> I love my dream
> I'll find the how…

Maybe you can take it from here?

41. ➡ New Pain Is Worse Than Old Pain

I HAVE A THEORY that one of the things that sends us scurrying back to our old patterns when we try something new is that new pain feels worse than old pain.

There are some kinds of pain that we are used to. We know the shape and the size and the likely duration of our old, familiar pain. For example, everyone has their particular health weakness — the one area of their body where illness is most likely to show up. For me, it's my lungs. If I'm going to get sick, it's probably going to be bronchitis. And over the years, bronchitis and I have gotten to know each other a bit. I know what it feels like and how long it will take to get better. So bronchitis doesn't frighten me.

I also have a cast-iron stomach, so the one time I got indigestion I honestly thought I might have to go to the emergency room. I didn't know what this new pain was, and I didn't know how much worse it would get, and not knowing scared me. Luckily, a few pink tablets later, I felt just fine.

It stands to reason that when you start behaving in a new way, you will start getting new and different problems, and that can be deeply disconcerting. The trick is to stay curious. Remember, nothing bad is happening. And these new problems are calling you forward to be a better person, a more evolved version of yourself.

LITTLE CHANGES ACTION STEP: Write down the answers to these three questions:

1. What's a pain you know well?
2. What new pain feels worse because it's unfamiliar?
3. What new pain do you fear might come to you if you keep moving in the direction of your dreams?

42. ➤ The Middle Way

Some of your fears are well founded. You're right to be worried about offending the wrong people (although I'm quite in favor of offending the right people). You're right to be concerned about your reputation. And as we discussed in chapters 5 and 13, it is just good sense to be concerned that people might find you selfish. But if you've spent your whole life giving to other people, your selfish-o-meter might be a bit out of whack. So here is a little exercise that is very simple and completely revolutionary. (Check out the free video of me walking you through this exercise step-by-step at www.StartRightWhereYouAre.com.)

Step 1

Answer each question with a single adjective. If more than one adjective comes to mind, put it on a separate line.

1. What are you afraid people might think about you if you were really successful?
2. What are you afraid people might think about you if you failed, publicly?
3. What is the last thing in the world you would want anyone to say about you?
4. What is a quality you deplore in others?
5. What unsavory quality do you secretly suspect might be true about you?

Step 2

Good work. Now, draw three columns and list the adjectives in the first column. So your list might look like mine:

What I Don't Want to Be		
bossy		
stupid		
cruel		
intolerant		
selfish		

If any of these negative adjectives provoke a strong reaction in you, you may want to make some 5-Minute Art about it in order to uncover the origin of your resistance. There could be a great teaching story in there, and simply bringing it to light could liberate you quite a bit.

Step 3

Now, skip the second column (for now) and write the most extreme version of the *absence* of each word in the third column. You may feel an urge to come up with the opposite, which could work, but that's not quite what I'm looking for. Close your eyes and check in with yourself: "What do I feel the absence of this word is?" So when I imagine the extreme absence of *bossy*, I see a picture in my mind of someone who refuses to assert herself at all, and the name I give that is *pushover*. And when I imagine the extreme absence of *intolerant*, I imagine a gate that is wide open, letting everything in all at once, and the name I give that is *indiscriminate*.

So now your sheet might look like this:

What I Don't Want to Be		The Extreme Absence of What I Don't Want to Be
bossy		a pushover
stupid		a supergenius
cruel		too nice
intolerant		indiscriminate
selfish		overgiving, a martyr

Step 4

Now comes the magical part. Ask yourself, "What word or phrase is somewhere in between these two words? What's the moderate, reasonable middle?" Again, don't ponder, and be sure to use words, images, or phrases that are evocative for you.

Now your sheet might look like this:

What I Don't Want to Be	The Middle Way	The Extreme Absence of What I Don't Want to Be
bossy	calmly assertive	a pushover
stupid	clever enough to get the job done	a supergenius
cruel	bringing down the hammer of sunshine	too nice
intolerant	judicious	indiscriminate
selfish	available during office hours	overgiving, a martyr

Your new way to handle your life is to let that middle column be in charge.

When I first came up with this exercise, I was struggling with feeling exhausted from overgiving and not wanting to be selfish. I wanted to be generous and supportive and available to people, and I didn't want to seem cold or withholding or shut down or unavailable. So finally I asked, in between overgiving and undergiving, what's the middle? And I thought, "The middle is 'office hours.'" The minute I thought that, a whole new world opened up to me. I thought, "Right. I can be giving and available during office hours. After 6:00 PM and on weekends, I'm not available." And that felt great to me.

I once got a question from Alison, who sold hand-batiked scarves and clothing. She was feeling the need to focus more on revenue, but she didn't want to seem too "sales-y." "Okay," I said. "Too sales-y is on one side. And what's the absence of too sales-y?" "Broke!" she exclaimed. "Not selling anything. No income." So, I asked, what's in the middle? "Offering my work to people who already love it. Maybe I could make a special offer to past customers. That doesn't feel sales-y. That feels like doing them a favor. That feels nice."

Another time I had a client in Vermont named Don who was a healer. He wanted to get the word out about his work, but he didn't want to seem pushy. When I asked him what the absence of "pushy" was, he laughed and said, "Napping, laying down on the job." And when I asked him what was in between "pushy" and "laying down on the job," he replied that he got an image in his mind of an outstretched hand. "Maybe," he said, "I could just reach out to one person — maybe to one journalist or to one influencer." That felt so simple and good to him that he made "the outstretched hand" part of his daily business practice. I recently saw him featured as an expert in a global telesummit. Clearly his outreach efforts are paying off.

Finally, just so you don't think this only applies to entrepreneurs, I had a friend who was reentering the dating world after her seventeen-year marriage ended. She was telling me how she didn't want to seem like a prude, but she didn't want to come off as overly available, either. When I asked her what was in the middle of those two things, she said, "A warm smile." And then she smiled so warmly, I knew she wasn't going to be single for long.

LITTLE CHANGES ACTION STEP: What new "middle way" policy can you enact today? (A tip of the hat to Buddhism for letting me borrow the term *middle way*.)

43. ➡ Being Decisive

LOOKING BACK OVER YOUR LIFE, do you feel like you've mostly made good decisions? I bet you have. With the exception of a few real clunkers — and we all have a few of those — you can trust yourself to make good decisions, most of the time. So go ahead and start making more decisions, faster. In the business world it is often said that "money loves speed." And it's true. The faster you can make decisions and execute them, the more likely you are to succeed. Better yet, if it turns out your idea is a big failure, then it's great to know that as quickly as possible.

The other nice thing about making decisions is that you can always make another decision. So if it turns out you have misjudged, or perhaps you didn't have all the information to begin with, you can regroup and, if necessary, pivot. Dithering never helped anything.

> The nice thing about making decisions is that you can always make another decision.

I was reading a beautiful tribute in *Vanity Fair* magazine to one of my heroes, Mike Nichols. He was part of the Nichols and May comedy team in the early days of Second City, which is my comedy alma mater, and he went on to direct some of the great films and theater productions of our time, including *The Graduate*, *Who's Afraid of Virginia Woolf?*, *Angels in America*, and *Working Girl*. He was an insightful, intelligent, sophisticated man and a comic genius. The playwright and screenwriter Tom Stoppard shared this reminiscence about him: "I was sitting in the stalls, and a stagehand walked in with a chair in either hand, and he shouted to Mike, Which chair? And Mike instantly said, That one, indicating the one in his left hand. As the guy walked off, I was thinking, Christ, I'll never be a director. The chairs weren't that different, you know, and I said, What was it about that chair? He said, Nothing, you just have to answer instantly — you can change your mind later."*

You will be perceived as better leader — perhaps even a great leader — if your people feel they can rely on you. Everyone, from your kids to your team to your church choir, will feel more comfortable if you make swift, powerful decisions.

LITTLE CHANGES ACTION STEP: Make a decision right now.

---

* Sam Kashner and Charles Maslow-Freen, "Mike Nichols's Life and Career: The Definitive Oral History," *Vanity Fair*, September 2015, www.vanityfair .com/hollywood/2015/09/remembering-director-mike-nichols.

44. ➡ That Little Kid Looks So...

SOMETIMES IT DOESN'T MATTER WHAT WE DO, our early programming will not release us. Even when you understand there is wisdom in taking care of yourself first, in letting go of perfectionism, and in allowing you and your work to be more visible in the world, the deeply ingrained messages that you received as a child just will not let you change the way you're behaving. This is a tough stage in personal development, or in any learning process: when you understand the ideas intellectually, but you can't quite seem to implement the ideas in your life.

One way to bridge the gap between theory and practice is to use imagination, storytelling, and a bit of dream magic.

What follows is an imagination game that evolved out of work I did with my friend and mentor, the wise and wonderful Sam Christensen, and his life-changing Image Design Process. You might enjoy accessing the audio version of me talking you through it at www.StartRightWhereYouAre.com so that you can just close your eyes, relax, and let the mental images play out. But just reading it should work fine, too.

Now, I know some of you are rolling your eyes and feeling sort of annoyed by these kinds of imagination games. That's fine. You're allowed to dislike it. But I encourage you to try it anyway. And some of you may start, but then feel, "I can't think of anything," or "I'm drawing a blank." That's fine. Don't push yourself to think of anything, just let the ideas sort of bubble up. And if nothing bubbles up, then fine. Maybe something will bubble up later tonight or in the shower tomorrow. Even one little bubble can be valuable.

Let's start by doing our 4:7:8 breathing. Feel your center, your heartwood, feel the spokes of energy radiating out from you. Relax your hands, your jaw, the bottoms of your feet. Good. Now I want you to imagine yourself to be somewhere very beautiful and peaceful — a real place or an imaginary place. And I want you to call to mind a photograph of you as a child. Maybe it lives in a scrapbook, or maybe it's on somebody's mantel, but the first picture of you under the age of ten that comes to mind is the right one.

And for now, just gaze at that photograph of that little kid and mentally complete this sentence: "Gosh, that little kid looks so _____." Whatever word comes to mind is perfect. As you're gazing at that photo, that little kid comes to life, and you can see them playing and interacting with the world. Just observe that kid for a moment, and notice what you see.

As you watch, you realize that you happen to know that this little kid has a very amazing special power. What is that kid's secret power? Again, just allow the answer to appear in your mind.

Here are some examples of a secret power:

the power to invent wonderful stories
the power to hear music that other people don't hear
the power to become invisible when you need to
the power to forgive, every single time
the power to be kind
the power to know exactly the right thing to say when someone's upset
the power to be stubborn
the power to fight for what's right

the power to make Dad laugh

the power to pretend you don't need or want anything

the power to fit in with the other kids, even when you know
   you're different

the power to talk to animals and plants

the power to pretend you don't care

the power to deliberately not notice when people are mean

the power to not tell the truth about what you see

the power to know when grown-ups are lying

the power to always work hard and push through no matter
   what happens

the power to always come to the rescue

the power to be weak, get sick, or need rescuing (so someone
   else can feel strong)

the power to create a distraction by getting into trouble

the power to be the best little girl ever

the power to be the best little boy ever

the power to refuse to play by the rules

the power to survive on crumbs

the power to escape to dreamland

the power to tiptoe because Mommy's resting

the power to be entertaining

the power to believe in wishes no matter what

You may notice that when this child engages their special power, the adults in the world have a response. For example, if this little kid's special power is knowing when grown-ups are lying, that might anger the adults, or it might make them burst out laughing. Notice what messages this little kid gets about their special powers. Notice, too, what does this little kid want but not get? How has this child learned to negotiate the world?

What else do you notice about this little kid?

And let's imagine now that the little kid notices you and greets you. How does the little kid greet you? With a casual wave or a warm hug? It turns out that the kid is impressed that you (the grown-up you) has accomplished something or has done something or is a certain way. What is it about you that really impresses this little kid? How do you feel about that?

Now the little kid gives you a gift that you didn't know you needed. Go ahead and open that gift. Notice whatever you notice about it. Say thank you. Put it somewhere safe.

You also have a gift for the little kid. Go ahead and give the little kid your gift. And imagine how the kid accepts your gift and says thank you.

If there's any other exchange that needs to happen or anything else that needs to be said or heard, let that unfold. Good. And now we're going to come back to this time and space, knowing that we can revisit that safe space with that little kid any time we want. Do one more round of 4:7:8 breathing and return to yourself.

Please make some notes about your experience.

The photo I remembered was _____.

I thought, "That little kid looks so _____."

I noticed, too, that the little kid was very _____.

My little kid's secret power was _____.

The adults' response to that secret power was _____.

The way in which the little kid negotiated the world was

_____.

My little kid was impressed that the adult me was

_____.

The gift my little kid had for me was _____.

The gift I gave my little kid was _____.

Other things I want to remember about this exercise are

_____.

Now, your response to this exercise might be fairly mild. An "Oh, that's interesting" or "Oh, that's sort of charming" reaction is not uncommon. And perhaps you got a little gem of an idea. Maybe the word you used to complete the sentence "Gosh, that little kid looks so _____" turns out to be a useful and powerful adjective. Perhaps it's a word you could use the next time you have to talk about yourself or your work. For others, this exercise can bring up strong emotions. If it's stirring up old stuff, then this is a great opportunity to make some 5-Minute Art.

Many of us are not members of the Happy Childhood Club. But the good news is that we're grown-ups now, and we get to re-parent ourselves. That's kind of what this work is about, learning how to become a better parent to yourself — how to be firm when you need to be firm, how to be loving and compassionate and respectful toward yourself, but not let yourself get away with anything, either.

> Many of us are not members of the Happy Childhood Club. But the good news is that we're grown-ups now, and we get to re-parent ourselves.

Yep. You and that little kid have been through a lot. And it's nice to take the opportunity to notice how beautiful that kid is, how unique that kid is, and to notice how much of that kid's energy is still in you.

Sheryl, one of my clients, remembered during this exercise that as a child she loved to write, but her writing mostly went unnoticed and unsupported by her family. Nevertheless, she always kept a diary. She said, "Until this exercise, I never saw all those years of diaries as my adaptive behavior. How clever of me. On the downside, I also learned to keep my creative efforts secret for fear of rejection, disapproval."

I might draw a few other lessons for Sheryl here. First, you don't need anyone's approval to do your art. After all, you did it without other people's approval for all those years. So now you could consider putting your work out there without being too concerned about their approval, especially when you think of all the kids who didn't have your tenacity — the now-grown-up kids who need to read your writing because they couldn't write it themselves. Finally, you learned an adaptive pattern of hiding that's no longer serving you. So we say, "Thank you, hiding. Thank you for teaching me about hiding. Now I'm going to go over here and explore what it's like in the spotlight."

Little Changes Action Step: Draw a picture of you as that little kid, and be sure to include your special power.

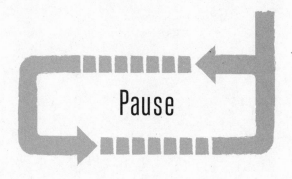

Pause

Too Much

Dear God,

My whole life I feel I have been told that I cannot be the person that I am.

Too sensitive.

Too colorful.

Too loud.

Too quiet.

Too much and somehow not enough.

Today, with your strength, I claim myself.

I inhale and allow my body to know its own strength; I exhale and feel my spirit glow.

I'm stepping out of the shadows into your bright, loving, all-seeing light.

Thank you for keeping the light on.

Love,

Me

45. ➡ Five Ughs and Three Ahhs

LET'S SAY YOU WAKE UP in the morning and notice that your nightstand is cluttered with old tissues, a half-empty water glass, and a big stack of books that you continue to believe that you'll read as soon as you get the time. You think, "Ugh."

After showering, you glare at your overstuffed closet, trying to find something that both fits and is remotely appropriate. You end up putting on pretty much the same outfit you always wear. You think, "Ugh."

In the car on the way to work, you notice that the little trash bin that you put in your car to restrain the empty pop bottles and other junk is overflowing, and there are crumbs in every crevice. You think, "Ugh." Cluttered desk. "Ugh." Overdue bill found on cluttered desk. "Ugh."

I believe that five ughs can unbalance your whole day. No individual ugh is a big deal, but all of them together add up to a sense of futility that is hard to overcome, especially when you are a procrastinator, an overachiever, or a perfectionist.

Now, let's say you wake up to a clean, welcoming environment. Maybe there's a little posy of fresh flowers on your bedside table. You might think, "Ahh." And what if your closet is filled with contemporary clothes (not necessarily trendy, but just right for your current life), all of which fit? "Ahh." And what if your car has been cleaned out and is in good repair? "Ahh."

Three ahhs trump any ugh. If you can start your day with three high-quality ahhs, the mountain of paper on your cluttered desk will not seem so insurmountable, and you might find it easy to make a peaceable call to your creditor, explaining your oversight and seeing if anything can be done about that pesky late fee.

The ahhs bring you a little jolt of happiness. They make you feel capable and in control and remind you of the beauty in the world. An ahh can come from anywhere: the way the light comes through your white linen curtains, the strength in your limbs when you do your twenty-minute workout, a good haircut, a love note in a lunch box, or a shower shelf that is clean because it has had all of the old, half-used bottles of product and ancient bath salts cleared away.

Three ahhs trump any ugh.

Five ughs vs. three ahhs is at the heart of the idea that little changes can make a big difference. You don't need to move to a new house, or lose five pounds, or quit your job in order to find the joy in your life. But if you make finding the joy in your life a priority, the easy way to your new house, healthier body, and better work opportunity will begin to reveal itself.

LITTLE CHANGES ACTION STEP: Find an ugh in your immediate area and fix it. (Not sure where to begin? You can start with getting rid of that dried-out pen that's been there for ages.)

46. ➼ Consider Future Costs, Not Sunk Costs

YOU'RE A SENTIMENTAL CREATURE, aren't you?

You love your memories, your stuff, and your attachments to people, places, and things. Those attachments make up the connections that give our lives meaning. But sometimes an attachment becomes less of a lifeline and more of a snare. How do you know when it's time to let go?

Economists everywhere sink their heads into their hands when they try to get us mortals to understand the fallacies that crop up around sunk costs. A sunk cost is the unrecoverable investment you have already made in a thing, a project, or a relationship. All too often we let the fact that we have already invested a substantial amount in something cause us to hang on to it, or, worse yet, continue investing in it. Our reasoning can sound like, "I know it's time to get rid of this expensive suit that I never wear, but I spent so much on it, I feel like I have to keep it." This is fallacious thinking. The money you spent on the suit is gone. It's over. You are not getting that money back no matter what you do, so stop letting the now-irrelevant thought that it was expensive influence your next decision. It might help you to pretend the suit was free. Then you might think, "I can't wait to give away this nice suit that's hardly been worn. It'll be great to have more space in my closet." That, my friends, is a rational decision.

(Feeling the urge to argue with me that the suit wasn't free, so my example is faulty? Try this instead: you've also got some items that were a great deal and that you wear all the time, right? So on average, you're coming out ahead. Plus, we all make wardrobe judgment calls, and not every outfit can be a winner. Give yourself a break already.)

Our reasoning about a sunk cost can also sound like, "Well, I've already spent three years getting this doctoral degree, so I guess I should see it all the way through, even though I'm absolutely hating it." Nope. The fact that you are miserable now is the information that matters. You're not getting those three years back, no matter what decision you make next. So it might serve you better to remember that no learning is ever wasted, in the same way that no time is ever wasted. You can't waste time. Time just happens, with or without you.

> You can't waste time. Time just happens, with or without you.

I'm always surprised when people say things like, "I got a law degree, but I never bothered to pass the bar, so I don't use it. It was a total waste." How can that be? You had the experience of getting a law degree, and I'm sure that influenced you mightily then, and continues to shape your worldview now. Just because you didn't get the result you thought you would doesn't mean it wasn't a valuable experience.

Relationships can exceed their natural life span when you focus too much on sunk costs, too. Staying married to someone for the sole reason that you've already been married for a long time is poor problem solving. You must consider your future costs, not your sunk costs. You can't get back the years you've spent, but what will it cost you to spend more years together? What opportunities would you be missing out on?

The past is the past, but it can help us make smarter decisions about the future. The final test for sunk costs is this: "Knowing what I know now, would I choose this again?" If the answer is no, then you have your decision.

So if you have items in your house that make you feel tired when you look at them, remember that you need only the stuff that is appropriate to your life as it is right now. The clothes that don't fit, the family heirlooms that take up too much space, and the treadmill that you never used much to begin with — these are all items that need to go. If it makes you feel better, take a photo of the stuff you're nostalgic about and keep it in your scrapbook. But all that stuff represents trapped energy, and the minute you release it, I promise you will feel lighter, healthier, and more free.

If there are people in your life who drain your energy, remember that not everyone who enters your circle is meant to stay there forever. I've heard it said that "some people come into our lives for a reason, and some for a season," and once that reason ceases to exist, or the season has ended, you owe it to both of you to let those people go. There's no need to be rude or abrupt about this. Be gracious and loving. Bless them and release them.

Maybe you have an old identity that you are ready to shed, and it's time for you to evolve. Stepping into a new identity can feel risky, but it is sometimes essential to your continued health and well-being. Sometimes new identities happen *to* you — you get fired, you get divorced, you become an empty nester — and it's a shock to the system. And sometimes the change is self-initiated, which, in a way, can feel even more shocking. You suddenly find yourself becoming an entrepreneur, a spiritual seeker, a public figure...and you may notice that not everyone in your life is thrilled by your new interests. That's okay. You don't need to cut those people out of your life (unless it's time for that — see above); just find other topics of conversation. Don't try to get support from people who are not capable of supporting you. Don't go to the empty cookie jar. Just step gracefully — or stumble awkwardly — into your new self, honoring the old self as you pass by.

As much as we love security, sameness, and stability, we hunger equally for change, novelty, and growth. Keep the balance, and you will discover a life that both honors your past and embraces your future.

LITTLE CHANGES ACTION STEP: Think of a situation in your life that needs a change, and ask yourself, "Would I make the same decision today, knowing what I know now?" Take one action based on your response.

47. ➡ The Seven Kinds of Clutter Nobody Ever Talks About

WHETHER WE'RE TALKING ABOUT CLUTTER that's physical, paper, electronic, or mental, its defining characteristic is that it's stuck. You can tell it's clutter because there's no movement, no progress, and no life — it's just the same old story over and over again. If you have a lot of stuff but it's in movement — for instance, you actually wear all of those clothes or use all that kitchen equipment, or the piles of paper on your desk are being handled, worked on, and pruned each day — then that's not clutter. That's just having a lot of stuff. Which is fine. You're allowed to have all the stuff you want.

> You can tell it's clutter because there's no movement, no progress, and no life — it's just the same old story over and over again.

Much of the advice about getting rid of clutter seems to start with the cheerfully abrupt command to "Just do it!" But when you can't identify the underlying beliefs that are causing you to become buried in clutter, that's almost impossible. So I've listed a few of the root causes of clutter that rarely get discussed and a few tough-love strategies to initiate change.

1. Nostalgia. You love the memory. You love the person who gave it to you. You love the size you were when you bought it. None of these is a good reason to hang on to something you're not using. Savor the emotion, make some 5-Minute Art about it, take a picture of it, and let it go.

2. *Your fantasy about your future life.* "Someday…" Yes, maybe someday. But not now. You don't yet have a mountain cabin to decorate, so the moose head can go. You don't yet have the sailboat, so the plastic tumblers with the cute anchors on them can go. You don't have the time right now to turn that pile of old T-shirts into a quilt, so they can probably go, too. And if all this rough talk is causing you pangs, that is excellent news. Those pangs mean that you really want that fantasy future to come true. So then take a step toward that today. Start a penny jar for the down payment on the cabin, book an afternoon sail for this weekend, or start cutting the quilt squares this evening.

3. *Future scarcity.* "I might need this sometime." Yes, you might. In which case you can go get another one then. I think this belief is actually a form of perfectionism in disguise: we perfectionists feel we must be prepared for every eventuality. This is an understandable and admirable goal but still no reason to hang on to something that's just taking up space. Also, if you are going to let an imaginary future make your decisions for you, why not imagine a future in which *not* hanging on to whatever it is turns out to be the best possible decision?

4. *Loyalty.* There are few things more pleasing to a human person than the feeling of being in the right, and few things less pleasing than the feeling of being in the wrong. Sometimes you don't want to get rid of clutter because it feels like admitting you made a mistake in buying this thing, that you misjudged. You want to believe in your past decisions, so you keep recommitting to those decisions long after they've been proved erroneous.

For example, you thought the yellow curtains would look great in the guest room, but they don't, so you've never put them up. And now every time you see them in the bottom of the linen cupboard, you think, "I really thought those would look nice, but they don't." And then, to keep from feeling as though you miscalculated, you think, "Maybe they'll look nice somewhere else someday." My mentor David Neagle did me a big favor when he taught me Leland Val Van de Wall's quote, "The amount of success you achieve will be in direct proportion to the amount of truth you can accept about yourself without running away." The ability to calmly accept that sometimes you blunder will hasten your spiritual maturity and probably improve your decorating skills.

5. Anthropomorphizing. As a child, I believed that things had feelings. I remember giving extra good-night kisses to my stuffed Dumbo when he was new, because he had missed out on all the kisses I had given my other beloved wubbies over the years, and I wanted him to catch up. (*Wubbies* is my family's word for all baby blankets, teddy bears, or special cuddle toys that a child loves especially and refuses to sleep without.) Well, I still believe that things have feelings. I thank my car for its faithful service, I express gratitude to English muffins for being so delicious, and I usually say goodbye to the house as I leave it, even if I'm just dashing out to run errands. I was recently near tears at the thought of replacing some old dish towels, because I felt it was disrespectful to all their years of hard work. If you're feeling simpatico, then try making some 5-Minute Art about the thing. Then, say thank you to the thing and ask someone else to get rid of it for you. Just because you're willing to say goodbye doesn't mean you have to be the one to deliver it to the thrift store or, worse yet, the dumpster.

6. Replaying old tapes. Worry is mental clutter. So is repetitive self-criticism. Any other thoughts that never lead to an outcome or a new thought are just taking up space in your head. It's important to your continued growth to distinguish between actual thinking and those old tapes.

Whenever you catch yourself running old tapes, clap your

hands loudly, or start to sing an uplifting song out load. Perhaps you can imagine the old thought falling deep into the earth where it can be composted. You can also interrupt your own pattern by yelling out an unusual phrase like, "Peeny-Weenie Woo-Woos!" and then force yourself to think of something else. (A *Peeny-Weenie Woo-Woo* is a fairly horrible cocktail that has achieved legendary status in my family, as its effects caused several of the normally quite reserved adults to get down on the floor and leg wrestle.)

7. The law of diminishing returns. The first one was great, and the second one was even better. But now you're on your fifth, and the thrill is wearing off. Whether we're talking about collectibles, books about space exploration, or red cashmere sweaters, take a look at the redundancies in your life, and see if there are a few items in the collection that can go.

When you are an expert on something, you tend to see minute variations as highly significant. Luke, a musician, composer, and teacher who is, at this writing, getting a PhD in music theory, informs me that his Telecaster and his short-scale Telecaster are completely different guitars, although I cannot really tell them apart. But he's the expert, and he really does play them both. By the same token, I have six varieties of black high-heeled shoes in my closet, and they each serve a very different purpose. If you are enough of a shoe-lover to actually be using all your black high-heeled shoes, then that's not clutter — that's just having good taste. But if you are only using one or two, you can probably afford to let the rest of the throng go.

Little Changes Action Step: Get rid of something. Anything. Right now.

48. ➥ Clutter Dive

HERE ARE A FEW QUESTIONS that might help you change how you think about clutter. Feel free to run any "stuck" situation, mental or physical, through these questions, and see what shifts for you.

1. Name an area of your life that you would really like to declutter.

2. What do you usually say to yourself about this issue? What's your "old tape" about it? In other words, what is your mental clutter about your clutter?

3. What is genuinely good about this stuckness? What is a real and true benefit to the situation staying the way it is? For example, as much as you might like to reorganize the basement, that is a time-consuming job, and you're enjoying spending that time on other projects right now. Or perhaps, while you deplore your overflowing broom closet, you sort of enjoy having an endless supply of reusable grocery bags. Acknowledging the blessing in the situation might make it clearer to you why you haven't changed it yet, and how you might approach the change in a way that doesn't sacrifice the good stuff.

4. What virtue or value is reflected in not *getting rid of this clutter?* For example, you might feel that holding on to an expensive household gadget that you don't use, because getting rid of it would mean that you wasted money, endows you with the virtue of thriftiness. Hanging on to nostalgia-laden items might speak to your value of family or love. It can be freeing to remember that you can be thrifty, family-focused, and loving while still having a clean closet. In fact, decluttering might even enhance that quality, value, or virtue in your life.

5. What is one thing you don't *want to have to do regarding your "stuck" thing? What are you resisting?* Clearing out the garage may mean that you have to have a conversation with your ex about the boxes that are stored there. Selling the antique platter may mean a trip into the city to get it appraised. Emptying the kids' rooms may mean finally facing the fact that they really have grown up and left.

Getting clarity on what's holding you back might help you to see a new way forward. Maybe someone could call your ex for you, or maybe there's a way to make that trip into the city a bit of a holiday. And going deeper into your feelings around your children's transition into independence might free you up in ways you never expected.

6. If this problem were to disappear right now, what would you have? Do you want what the absence of this problem will give you? Sometimes we hang on to familiar problems because if the old problem really did go away, we'd be forced to face some other, bigger problem. And as we've discussed, old pain can feel preferable to new pain.

Clearing off the patio might reveal the fact that the whole thing really needs to be repaved. On the other hand, if the patio were decluttered, you might be able to host a barbecue, and the idea of that party might just be the motivation you've been waiting for.

7. Who else is involved in this? Is there a power struggle or emotional conflict with a person (living or dead) that's keeping this situation tied in knots? Stuff is hardly ever just stuff; it represents our story about our past. I remember one particularly tall, dark, and handsome fellow in one of my live workshops who admitted that he would love to get rid of the piano in his living room, but he knew his wife would never agree. It had been a gift to her from a friend of hers who had died after a long illness, and he was certain she was too sentimental about it to let it go. Imagine how surprised he was when, on screwing his courage up to ask her about it, she eagerly agreed. Turns out the piano wasn't bringing her joy — it was only reminding her of her friend's last painful years and taking up a lot of space in which she'd really prefer to do her morning yoga. It's amazing what you can find out when you ask.

8. *Anything else you are noticing?* There are no right or wrong answers here, just whatever gets illuminated for you.

LITTLE CHANGES ACTION STEP: Make some 5-Minute Art about the story you tell about your clutter. Need a suggestion? Perhaps try a one paragraph fantasy/sci-fi story about a character named Beautiful House who gets trapped by Notorious Clutter, and cast yourself as the space hero who saves the day at the last minute.

49. ➡ Clearing Out Your Dream Closet

I WAS HAVING LUNCH ONE DAY with my friend Colleen Gallion, the wonderful executive coach, and we started joking around about the idea that all your childhood ambitions, youthful desires, goals, and old dreams for your life could be stored in an imaginary closet somewhere. Hers would have one of those horned Viking helmets to represent her dream opera career, and mine would have a pair of rainbow suspenders for my grade-school dream of being a mime. (Don't laugh. Mime is cool.)

Close your eyes and imagine what your dream closet would look like. Is it a storage locker? An airplane hangar? An entire Renaissance castle? Or just a little cubbyhole? And notice your dreams. What form do they take? Are they costumes? Boxes? Pieces of paper?

What does your dream closet look like?

As you poke around in this closet, you might find that some of your dreams really belong to someone else. Perhaps you have a dream of your mother's that got handed down to you. Are there some dreams that never fit you to begin with? Or a few that, while they might have been right at the time, now seem as hopelessly outdated as an old prom dress? And maybe there's anger there, or regret, or sadness around some of those dreams. Maybe there's a dream that would appreciate an apology.

As you sort through your dreams, do any of them have

anything to say to you? Are any of them fighting for attention? Are some of them dusty and lackluster? Maybe there's some immediate action you can take inside this closet. Maybe you can put a few dreams into the hall of fame, or maybe there are some that you're eager to release. (I like to imagine that old dreams just slide peacefully right into the Net's dream recycling system.) Maybe there are some dreams that are so fun you just have to keep them, no matter how far-fetched they seem. And there might be at least one dream that you want to take out and start experimenting with.

If your dream closet needs some immediate spring cleaning, you can blow the dust and clutter away and put some sparkle back in there. Make it look the way you want it to look, the way it deserves to look. And to the dreams that have fled, the ones that weren't right, the ones you're letting go of, say, "Thank you. Thank you for being my dreams. Go find your perfect person." And (*poof!*) release them.

The last time I led this exercise live, I was asked, "But if there's a stubborn dream in there, like the Prince or Princess Charming who never noticed you, but that you still dream about, how do you get rid of those?" A poignant question. I'm not sure that we're meant to get rid of those dreams of love entirely. Any memory of love, of being loved, is precious, and unrequited love has a special sweetness, because it has never been sullied by messy reality. (Remember your first crush on a pop singer or TV star? Was there ever a love so pure?)

What I would encourage you to release is the regret. It's easy to believe that things should be different, but as we discussed in chapter 33, there is no alternative reality in which you and Prince or Princess Charming got together. So release the belief that the past could or should be different, and perhaps focus instead on the desire that this dream is pointing to. What you may truly regret is the person you imagine you would have become if that relationship had flourished. So, who would you be if you were with Charming? Can you allow yourself to be that way today?

Little Changes Action Step: Make some 5-Minute Art about one of your favorite old dreams. Need a prompt? Write a monologue from the point of view of someone (you) who had achieved your dream. So mine might begin, "No one ever expects a mime to talk, but I've got a lot to say. Now, about those rainbow suspenders…"

50. → A Few Remarkably Destructive Communication Habits to Stop Right Now

SOME COMMUNICATION HABITS are both easy to fall into and shockingly destructive to your relationships, your mood, and your overall success, especially considering how common they are. Bringing your awareness to both what you are saying and how you are saying it can transform your world in some delicious ways.

1. Quit complaining. Right now. Permanently. Because it makes your face do ugly things, plus it just doesn't work. Complaining and her twin sister, nagging, are two very ineffective strategies. They do not contribute to good communication. You may have noticed that all of your nagging and complaining falls on deaf ears, and the more you complain, the more deaf others become. This is because when people feel defensive, they cannot hear very well. I'm no body language expert, but I have noticed that when the arms are crossed, the ears are closed.

These strategies also don't effect change. Nagging and complaining don't inspire vision, movement, or joy. They bring you down and keep you down. They are the rotten bananas in the fruit bowl of life.

The easiest way to quit complaining and nagging is to replace them with a request. So, rather than saying, "It makes me crazy that everyone is always late to the Monday

> The more you complain, the more deaf others become.

team meeting," you could say, "I'd like to request that we all be in the room five minutes early next week. Is everyone willing to commit to that?" For extra oomph, you can also add an incentive, such as "I'll even bring in donuts and kale chips!"

2. Admit that you're not really "frustrated." I have noticed that some people say they are frustrated, when clearly, they're really furious. "No, I'm not mad. I'm not. I'm just…frustrated," they fume.

Frustration is the combination of anger and impotence. So the next time you catch yourself saying that you feel frustrated, ask yourself, are you angry? If so, what can you do so that anger knows it's been felt? And are you truly impotent? Chances are you have more power in the situation than you're allowing yourself to exercise. On the other hand, if you truly are impotent, then you might as well relax. There's no sense in burning energy over something you cannot control. That's like getting mad at the rain.

3. Don't apologize when you haven't done anything to be sorry for. You apologize when someone bumps into you. You apologize when you're afraid. You apologize to defuse someone else's anger. You apologize when you are not even a little bit sorry.

Apologizing gets increasingly ineffective the more it gets used. Stop apologizing for everything you think you've done incorrectly. Say thank you instead. Rather than saying, "I'm sorry for bothering you with this," say, "Thank you for taking the time to work with me on this." Instead of saying, "I'm sorry it took me so long to respond to you," you can say, "Thank you for being patient."

4. And if you really are sorry, say it and mean it. Be specific about what, exactly, you are sorry for. Claim responsibility and ask for compassion, understanding, and forgiveness. Demonstrate that you are changing your behavior.

Ask if the person will accept your apology. Ask if they will accept your amends. Whether the answer is yes or no, let it drop. It's over. Be done with it.

LITTLE CHANGES ACTION STEP: Identify another communication habit that could be getting in your way. Perhaps you have a habit of phrasing statements as questions (uptalk), or inserting minimizing qualifiers into your speech or writing, like, "I don't know if this is right," or "I have this little idea." You might be overusing the word *just*, as in, "I just wanted to ask you if..." Or maybe you allow yourself to interrupt others.

51. ➤ No More Rehearsing Conversations

No more rehearsing conversations in your head.

No more replaying old conversations.

No more playing revised versions of old conversations.

No more telling the story of what happened.

You have a wonderful imagination. And your acting is pretty good, too. (Yes, that's what you're doing when you're making speeches to someone who isn't there about something that's not actually happening.) When you get nervous or upset about the future, your imagination wants to create all kinds of pictures and scenarios so you can "rehearse." But ask yourself, has any of that rehearsal ever helped you in the moment? Have you ever been able to use that wonderful dialogue? Has rehearsing a moment or a conversation ever helped you get what you wanted out of the situation? Me neither.

> When you are trapped inside your own head, it becomes very difficult for you to focus on anything outside it.

A certain brand of narcissism is born of anxiety. When you are trapped inside your own head, it becomes very difficult for you to focus on anything outside it. So you miss important conversational cues, and you ignore the energy of the room. You are disconnected. This is not helpful if you are seeking connection.

Now, for professional actors, rehearsal is part of the job. But as an actor, I found myself twisted into knots before every audition, trying to anticipate what might happen and what I might say, above and beyond the script. Here's what I started repeating instead: "Divine intelligence tells me all I need to know."

Perhaps I might have also said, "I trust the Net to support me," or "Nothing bad is happening."

Reminding myself to relax and receive information as it appears makes my life go more smoothly and eliminates much of the muzzy-headedness that comes with the adrenaline rush of anxiety and racing thoughts.

Maybe you aren't inclined to rehearse the future but find yourself rehearsing the past. We all have had conversations that stay with us — usually the ones where we didn't say what we wanted to say, or couldn't think of the right comeback, or were so upset that we failed to respond at all. And the desire to go back in time and speak our heart is strong. The French even have a phrase for it, *l'esprit de l'escalier*, which means "the spirit (inspiration) of the stairs" or "staircase wit." It's the perfect comeback that you think of once you are already out of the room and halfway out of the building. My friend the award-winning playwright Emilie Beck and I once cracked ourselves up by coining the phrase *le spectacle de la voiture*, which is the flawless audition you give in the car on the way home from the actual audition. But it is our pride that wants to turn back the clock, and it is our vanity that wishes for a do-over.

One more way of staying stuck in an old story is by continually retelling the story of how you have been hard done by. The lover who left, the ungrateful employer who ignored you, the time you were cheated, misled, or betrayed — these stories are deliciously dramatic, and if we tell them properly, we get to see ourselves as desirable but unloved, faithful but unrewarded, honest, trusting, loyal, and true.

The problem is that by retelling the stories of those old

injustices, you are keeping them alive. The injury happened only once, but you are causing it to happen over and over again. You are picking at a wound and refusing to let it heal.

Here are my suggestions for stopping these highly addictive thought habits:

1. Make some 5-Minute Art about any story that still rankles.

2. Stop telling the story, once and for all.

3. Do not give the situation any more energy. Anytime the thought creeps into your mind, you can shout my new favorite phrase, "Banana Pants!" or any energy-shifting words of your choice, and force yourself to think about something else. Sing an old camp song, compose a hilariously irrational rant about the tree in front of your house, ask someone else how they are doing — say anything that will distract you and re-root you in the present moment.

4. If you find that you cannot stop reciting imaginary conversations, consider saying them out loud and replacing all of the pronouns with *I* and *me*. So you might end up saying things like, "I can't believe I fired me." "I deserved to treat me so much better than I did." "I will always regret the day I left me." "I am never going to speak to me again!" (door slam optional). You may realize that you sound ridiculous, which is always a good place to start your healing. You may make yourself cry, which is another perfect new beginning. And by removing the *you* from the conversation, you can start to take complete responsibility for what happened and for your reactions to what happened. You can see more clearly the part you might

> You may realize that you sound ridiculous, which is always a good place to start your healing.

have played in creating that event and uncover a whole
new version of yourself.

LITTLE CHANGES ACTION STEP: Think of any situation from
your life that you wish had gone differently and replay part of the
conversation (the real one or an imaginary one) out loud, replacing all of the pronouns with *I* or *me*. Fun, right?

52. ➡ Greet Your Mistakes with Grace

FEAR OF CRITICISM is such a huge part of what's keeping you stuck, it deserves its own book. I often hear people say they're afraid of failure, but I suspect that if they could fail in secret, they would actually be okay with that. It's the public nature of failure that terrifies us.

If we had had perfect parents, teachers, guardians, and coaches growing up, our mistakes and failed efforts would have been met with loving understanding, encouragement, and a compassionate look at the important lessons learned. We would have learned to get curious about our errors rather than feeling ashamed of them.

And from here on in, you get to be a perfectly wonderful parent to yourself. You get to greet your mistakes with ease and grace. You get to cry it out, shake it off, and make note of what to do differently next time. You get to let yourself off the hook once and for all, and you get to quit punishing yourself (and everyone else) for your perceived failures.

If you learn to treat your failures as mere information rather than occasions for judgment, you will achieve true spiritual maturity.

If you learn to treat the failures of others as mere information rather than occasions for judgment, you will become what is officially known as a saint.

Meanwhile, understand that fear of criticism is, once again, the people-pleasing part of your survival instinct derailing you. From the standpoint of evolutionary biology, being concerned about what other people think makes perfect sense. You need to be approved of in order to stay alive. Being too weird could get you tossed out of the tribe. So you become understandably reluctant to put your work out into the world, for fear of harsh judgment and rejection.

I often have clients tell me, "Well, I would like to write a book, but I'm afraid someone might think I was too weird/too snooty/not good enough/whatever." And so then I say, "Okay, let me get this straight: you are allowing the imaginary opinion of an imaginary person who exists in an imaginary future decide whether or not you write the book that you haven't even started yet? Really?"

Look, if you're going to give power to an imaginary person, why not imagine a person who loves your work? Imagine someone who is passionately enthusiastic about what you do and who can't wait to tell all their friends. Doesn't that seem nicer?

> Let me get this straight: you are allowing the imaginary opinion of an imaginary person who exists in an imaginary future decide whether or not you do the thing that you haven't even started yet? Really?

LITTLE CHANGES ACTION STEP: Make some 5-Minute Art about a hurtful or humiliating experience (real or imagined) and see if you can find any of the humor, forgiveness, or compassion that might allow you to let it go. For example, you might write a folktale about a teacher who was put under an evil spell that caused her to tell innocent third-graders that they were completely untalented. Then the third-graders rebelled and sang a song of joy so loudly and with such conviction that the spell was broken, and the teacher apologized, and all the kids grew up believing in themselves. The End.

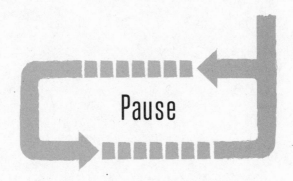

Pause

Not Exactly What I Had Planned

Dear God,

I have a story in my head about how my career was supposed to go.
I really thought my life would be different from this.
I mean, for a while there it was looking so promising, you know?
Frankly, I'm disappointed.
But I get it that to be disappointed is to be ungrateful.
And, come to think of it, faithless.
Ouch.
Okay. I am going to focus on the beauty of this life that you and I
   have created together.
And it is beautiful.
Especially without my story of "failure" or "not good enough" or
   "should be more successful" burying my joy.
Let's unearth all the joy we can.
And God, thank you for shining your light on my (brilliant) life
   that is unfolding (perfectly) in your divine time.

Love,
Me

53. ➡ Test-Drive a Bigger Goal

YOU'RE GETTING PRETTY GOOD at this "little changes, big difference" thing now, and maybe you're thinking you'd like to try a bigger goal. I'm all for it.

Let's start here:

1. Write down the name of a project you would like to do but feel stuck about.
2. Write down three reasons for not doing it, or three things that you are afraid might happen if you were to do this project.
3. Write down three possible good things that might come out of it. It doesn't matter how realistic these things are or how probable they are, it just matters that they are inside your mind.
4. Now, picture yourself having completed this project and realizing it's a big, fat failure. It just doesn't work. Make a picture of that in your mind and write down what you think it would mean about you if you were to fail at this project. Because the problem with failure is not so much the failure itself, it's what we make the failure mean.
5. Now imagine yourself doing this project and having it turn out to be a huge success, beyond your wildest dreams. Take a mental snapshot of what that might look like, and write down what you think that would mean about you.

Everyone has a unique response to this exercise, which is part of why I like it. There's no right answer — there's just your answer.

I had one client, a painter named Dawn, who realized that she had turned her failure to clean her house into a story about being a failure as a homemaker, a wife, a mom, and a human being. But when she imagined succeeding at cleaning her house, she wrote that it would mean that "I'm competent, I'm a grown-up, and I deserve to leave the house, to read a book, and to ride my horse." She confided that she hadn't ridden her horse in five months because she felt like she didn't deserve to do anything fun.

I suggested that she move horseback riding and book reading up to the top of her must-do list. After all, she'd already tried the approach of "Let's punish Dawn until she cleans her house," and it wasn't working. So now I suggested she try the strategy "Let's remind Dawn what a beautiful life she has. And let's make her so joyful that she doesn't give two figs about a dirty house, or she and the kids clean it as a group project, or she hires someone else to come in and do it, or she ends up just so plum happy from going riding that it's easy for her to do it."

During that same session, a writer named Gita had this insight: "When I asked what would happen if I failed, the thought immediately came, 'It would mean that I tried.' And when I asked what it would mean if the project was a huge success, I thought, 'Well, it would mean that I tried.' I can have the same results; it's just how I choose to look at it."

Rather than focusing on what it would mean about you if you fail, focus on what it would mean about you if you tried.

LITTLE CHANGES ACTION STEP: Imagine the end of Dawn's story. How do you think it turned out? What might happen for you if you gave yourself permission to do the things you love to do first and quit punishing yourself for not doing other things?

54. ➤ Life Does Not Move in One Direction

You think that if you get enough accolades, you'll be content. You could finally appreciate yourself. But that's a myth.

Name five of your most important accomplishments. You're in the ninety-fifth percentile of high achievers in that area, aren't you? And has that helped? Are you any less hard on yourself? Of course not.

All you see are the places you could be better, all the people who you think are doing better than you.

You think you're behind, but you're not. You're perfect.

The idea that life is a race and that you could somehow win or lose it is insane, but we keep telling it. Life is a road. Success is a ladder. Time is marching ever forward. But we know it's not true.

We are on shifting sands, sliding forward and backward and sideways and diagonally in our thinking, our feeling, our learning, and our lives.

Time swirls about us endlessly, effortlessly sweeping us back to that day in the third grade, that picnic by the lake, that long and horrible night. Certainly time is the most unreliable of all the unreliables. If we think of our lives as being linear, we cheat ourselves out of the fullness of our experience.

That foolish linear thinking is what leads to self-immolating thoughts like "I should be more successful by now" and "Look, that person is more successful than I am."

We know these thoughts are lies, too, but if you measure only by the clock, it is all too easy to slip those lies into your pocket and carry them around as part of your belief about yourself.

The more we learn about our art (our love), the less we know.

The longer we live on this earth, the more the years seem to pass in a day.

The more our fortunes rise and fall, the more we recognize that money and status are no more accurate markers of success than a new crop of tomatoes or a big hug from an eight-year-old.

LITTLE CHANGES ACTION STEP: For one second, notice the ways in which your life is a wonderful looping thing, intersecting with the Net in many different directions at once.

55. → You're Getting Paid in the Currency You're Asking For

MANY OF THE CLIENTS I work with feel chronically underappreciated. People say they love your work, but no one wants to pay full price. People say they appreciate you, but you still feel neglected. You feel like you are always in second place.

Here's what I notice: you're getting paid in the currency you're asking for. If you're not getting paid full price, you're probably not asking for full price.

If you are feeling neglected, there is something in your behavior that allows people to believe that it is okay with you if they neglect you. If you always come in second, you are somehow managing to position yourself perfectly to not quite win.

A few years into my business, I had a healthy list of email contacts who eagerly read and responded to my free materials, but my revenue was low. Then my wise friend Melissa pointed out that I very rarely offered anything for sale, and when I did offer a program or workshop, I was much too low-key about it. It was as though my sales strategy was something like "Okay, here's a bunch of stuff for free, and now by the way I've got something for sale, but you don't have to buy it if you don't want to, and now let's talk about something else, okay?" I was afraid that if I tried to sell them something, I would lose their affection. I had made their affection more important to me than income.

Consequently, I had a lot more love than money. My list was

giving me exactly what I had been asking for. Once I realized that I could ask for love and money and get both, and that offering workshops, products, and services was also an act of love, my income doubled and then tripled. That was fun.

So I invite you now to consider what currency you're getting paid in.

You may be asking for affection, as I was, or for appreciation. Your preferred currency could be social media "likes." It could be sex, or compliments, or security, or even the feeling of being underappreciated. It sounds weird, but there was a time in my life when it was kind of important to me that I work very hard and be both underpaid and underappreciated. A slight martyrdom complex, tinged with romantic ideals about sacrifice and excruci-atingly low self-esteem will do that to a person. Every time I felt neglected, it validated my belief that I was unworthy and unlovable, which felt familiar and comfortable. And I certainly preferred the well-known pain of feeling neglected to the unknown pain of asking for what I really wanted.

> Do you prefer the well-known pain of feeling neglected to the unknown pain of asking for what you really want?

This is how your self-concept affects the results you get in your life. And those results are showing you exactly where you need to grow, mature, and stretch.

Let me put this another way: I used to assume that the phrase "Thoughts become things" was one of those inconsequential aphorisms promising that if you can dream it, you can do it. But then I figured out that it is quite a literal statement. Check out this process:

Step 1. You have an idea. For example, you might have the idea "I could write a book."

Step 2. If your self-image agrees with the thought "I could write a book," then you start taking steps, and eventually you have the thing itself. You have a book.

Alternative Step 2. If, however, your self-image does not agree with the thought "I could write a book," and counters with some self-defeating thought like "Yes, but it's all been said before," or "I don't know how," then you *won't* take steps, and eventually you will have the no-thing that is no book.

So you think of a thing, and then you behave in a certain way, and then you get a certain result, and then you look at the results, and you say, "Well, I guess I can't do any better than that." And then you just keep reinforcing the thought, which reinforces the behavior, which reinforces the results, and that's how you stay stuck. Luckily, it is really easy to reverse-engineer this process and figure out what your problem might be. What are your current circumstances or results? How are those results a match for what you believe about yourself and the world? What new belief will allow you to create better results?

LITTLE CHANGES ACTION STEP: Play around with the idea that you are getting paid in the currency you're asking for because it matches your self-concept. Where does that idea take you?

56. ➤ Swatting Away Success

I USED TO BELIEVE that there wasn't really any such thing as a fear of success. I was wrong.

I see people deliberately keep themselves small. I see people create a crisis to divert energy away from a project that looks like it might be too successful. I see people keep their foot on the neck of their business so that it doesn't get too big. I've even seen people swat success away from them like it's an annoying fly.

I remember the time a designer named Jo was telling me how broke she was, and then in the next breath she was saying how someone had asked her if she offered gift certificates, and she had said no. Swat.

I explained to Jo, as patiently as I could, that gift certificates are basically free money and free customer acquisition. Think about it: someone wants to give you money and introduce your work to a new person, and all you have to do is write "gift certificate" on the back of a matchbook and hand it back to them. (Okay, you probably want to make it look a little nicer than a matchbook, but you see my point.)

Because Jo was committed to the story that she was broke and money is hard to get, she simply could not notice the opportunity to receive money easily.

Are you guilty of swatting away money, success, or love? Is there someone who's been offering to make an introduction for you? An opportunity to speak that you keep turning down because you feel too shy, or not "ready"? Is there a simple way for you to improve your revenue? Just think what the phrase "Do you want fries with that?" has done for McDonalds' bottom line over the years. Or is there a person you might be romantically interested in, if only you didn't keep rejecting the idea out of hand?

Sometimes you guarantee lack of success through inaction. I have a friend who got paid a lot of money for her book advance, so she invested some of that money in self-funding a book tour. She went all over the country holding events and readings, and drew in a lot of people. And it wasn't until she got home that it occurred to her that she had not bothered to get a single name or contact information from any of her audience members. She went to all the hard work to build her tribe, then she cut herself off from being able to reach them again and offer them more of her work. Swat.

Then there's good, old-fashioned avoidance. We make sure success cannot find us by refusing to make the phone call, send in the application, publish the ebook, or speak our mind. We don't keep our bodies in peak

> Sometimes you guarantee lack of success through inaction.

condition (or even base-camp condition), and we stop trying new things. We don't often think of not doing something as a decision, but it is. Not working on your creative projects is a decision to remain dissatisfied. Not asking for a raise is a decision to limit your income. Not keeping the car tuned up and in good repair is a decision to be in need of a new car. A delayed decision, and perhaps a passive decision, but nevertheless, you have chosen a course of action (inaction) that will result in a definite outcome. Want different results? Stop avoiding.

LITTLE CHANGES ACTION STEP: Write down one way in which you've swatted away money, success, or love, and take one all-new step toward welcoming those things instead.

57. ➠ An Antidote to the Fear

ABOUT THREE MONTHS BEFORE my book *Get It Done: From Procrastination to Creative Genius in 15 Minutes a Day* was to be released, I found myself in a mild panic. I was concerned about the book launch and managing all the opportunities and interviews. There are a million different things a person can do to promote a book, and I wanted to make sure I was picking the right things and doing them well. At the same time, I didn't want to take on too much. As it happens, "She Who Takes On Too Much" is my tribal name, so there was faint chance of my being under-scheduled.

During a meditation session, I got a little vision that helped me a lot then and that continues to comfort me. In my vision, it seemed as though I was in a giant circus tent, with all kinds of noise and activity around me. I was way up high on the high-wire platform, and I knew I had to step out onto the wire and walk across. This seemed impossible. Then I heard a calm, wise voice say, "Don't pay any attention to the circus. You can ignore all that." And suddenly I had blinders on and I put my head down, so I couldn't see very much of what was happening around me. I could only focus on my feet, and the next three or four feet of the wire. Then the voice said, "Put your hand on my shoulder, and I'll lead you across." Spirit took the form of a strong man who appeared in front of me. I put one hand on his shoulder, and he walked me across the wire, one step at a time. Halfway through I started to panic, and the voice said, "You wouldn't be afraid to walk on this wire if it were only a few inches off the ground, would you? The trick is to just not notice how high up you are."

This idea that I truly didn't have to pay attention to anything that was not in my direct field of vision, but rather could just keep my head down and do the next step that was in front of me while trusting that I was being guided and led, was deeply reassuring. My mantra became "Be grateful, stay calm, and take care of business."

> The trick to navigating the high wire is to just not notice how high up you are.

LITTLE CHANGES ACTION STEP: If you had someone that you could trust leading you across the high-wire act of your life, who would it be? Picture that person or entity in your mind, and imagine what encouraging words they have for you right now.

58. → Will Success Make You Selfish?

I FIND THE IDEA that becoming successful will somehow turn you mean or selfish kind of funny. I get it — there are certainly enough stories about this in the culture. We all know the story in which someone has to learn a valuable lesson about not being so dazzled by the trappings of success that they forget what's really important (family, roots, authenticity, sincerity). But my experience is that people who are nice stay nice, no matter how rich or successful they become. And people who are thoughtful stay thoughtful. I think it's safe to say that if you're not selfish now, it's unlikely that you will become so.

> People who are nice usually stay nice, no matter how rich or successful they become.

What if success actually made you a better person? What if your success made you more loving? What if it made you more creative?

And let's look at the oft-held belief that rich people are bad, or stingy, or profligate. What if wealth allowed you to be even more supportive to the charities you love? If you had the ability to hire more people, even just to help around the house, you could be creating jobs in a great work environment for people, and thus bringing greater prosperity to more families in your community. If you spent more money, you could better support the small businesses, restaurants, and service people in your town. And if you made it to the top of your profession, per-haps then you could open the door of opportunity for others.

Try these statements on for size:

Success makes me more welcoming.

Success makes me more courageous.

Success makes me more gracious.

Success makes me more peaceful.

When I succeed, everyone around me benefits.

LITTLE CHANGES ACTION STEP: How would you like your suc-cess to influence you? Could you enact that change today?

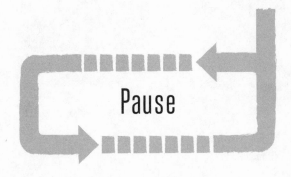

Pause

The Talent Box

Dear God,

It has been so long, I'm not sure I still have any talent at all.

I remember I used to be good at it.

I was good at it before I knew it was a talent. (I just thought everyone could do it.)

It came naturally to me. It was fun.

But that talent has been sitting in a box on a high shelf in the back of the closet for so long, I'm afraid it's no good anymore.

I'm afraid I'll look like a fool if I try.

I'm afraid I'll die without ever sharing my talent.

Being caught in between fear and fear, I am paralyzed.

Be still, you say, and know that I am God.

Okay, not paralyzed, but still. Stillness. Still.

In stillness I remember that you gave me this talent to begin with.

In stillness, I can reach up, blow the dust off of my talent and maybe just start to play around with it.

Just to experiment.

You know, God — this could be really fun.

Love,

Me

59. ➝ Your Tribe Is Looking for You

Now that we've got you firmly in the center of yourself and in the center of your life, and you're getting good at trusting your intuition, it's time to get you connected with other people: your tribe.

In his dazzling book *Far from the Tree*, Andrew Solomon points out that while we are all members of the tribes we are born into (part of our family, our geographical area, our native language, and our era), we also must seek out the tribe that celebrates our specialness. Just think of the first time you felt truly at home in a place that wasn't home. For me, it was in the theater. But maybe for you it was on the baseball field, or in the chess club, at Comic-Con, at a Grateful Dead concert, at the equestrian center, or out in the back alley behind the school.

I've heard there's a whole tribe of "Quackers" — middle-aged women who love the brightly colored, beaded, and appliquéd sweaters made by Quacker Factory. They wear their sweaters while traveling, so they can identify each other in airports, and they greet each other by saying "Quack, quack, quack." I love this so much I cannot tell you. I think there is a real lack of whimsy in the world (even if it's a kind of flat-footed whimsy), and I love it that there's a company that deliberately ignores fashion in favor of their

> Just think of the first time you felt truly at home in a place that wasn't home.

values of fun, silliness, and good, old-fashioned friendliness and still grossed over fifty million dollars in 2011. That is one terrific tribe.

When we unite with other like-minded people, we gain a power beyond ourselves. We gain insights, opportunities, and friendships. We suddenly have leverage — the ability to get a large return with only a small expenditure of energy. Let me give you an example: if you wanted to raise $25,000 for the charity of your choice, and you tried to do that from your own income or savings, it might be a struggle. It could happen, but most of us would probably have to donate $100 a month for over twenty years. But if you are part of a group of a hundred people who all believe in that charity, you could each donate $250 once and accomplish your goal in one month. And maybe twenty people out of that group of one hundred have access to even more funds, so they might be able to match the original donation, and now you've raised $50,000. And let's say that $50,000 starts to bring some attention to the charity, so more people are drawn to support it. Suddenly your $250 is being magnified by a tribe of other people: you are part of a movement.

Part of the problem you may have had in changing your life is that you've tried to do it all by yourself, or you've tried to do it with the wrong people. Finding your tribe will accelerate your transformation and will often give you the means for the kind of quantum leap that seems impossible to most people.

> The right tribe adores you, just as you are right now.

When you have the right tribe, it gets easier to find important resources like a great real estate agent or doctor. The right tribe can help you find a job, a spouse, a terrific pair of new black shoes. Better yet, you get to be of service to the tribe, offering your time and talents to a group that appreciates you. The right tribe adores you just as you are right now. The right tribe will be your cheerleaders, hold you accountable, and call you to be your better self.

The tribe I'm talking about is not your family, your friends, your officemates, or your current spiritual community. It's a group of people in your life who are dedicated to helping you shine your weirdo specialness into the world. These people may not care about the day-to-day details of your life, and they are not invested in your staying the same (which is usually what your family and friends want, because they want to keep you safe). This tribe will inspire you to be better, bolder, braver, and more genuinely yourself than you've ever been before.

Finding your tribe may feel like a tall order, but it's easier than you think. Especially now that we have the internet and you can connect with like-minded people all over the world, instantly.

Together with your tribe, you can change the world and change yourselves. But another reason it's important to have a tribe is to combat the epidemic of loneliness. Even as connected as we all are, people are more disconnected, too. We're not having those little chance conversations in line at the grocery store, or in doctor's offices or airports, because we're checking our phones. And the quality of the connectedness that we experience on our phones tends to be ephemeral, disappearing almost as quickly as it happens.

Sometimes you will feel alone in your life no matter what. And you must face your toughest struggles all by yourself. But a good tribe can stand by you during those trials and point the way to a brighter future.

For example, I love being a member of a tribe of teachers, authors, coaches, and healers who all care about conscious entrepreneurship. We convene in person once or twice a year, and many of us are in other, overlapping tribes, so we see each other fairly often. We also have a private Facebook group where we can ask questions, share heartbreaks, puzzle out moral dilemmas, and celebrate our wins. It's lovely to be part of a group of people who all believe that we can do well by doing good. We are also actively engaged in the larger questions that face the personal development industry — Does what we do really help people? How do we know if it does or doesn't? What are our metrics for success? — and ethical issues of pricing, intellectual property (it can get a little sticky when there's no copyright on wisdom), false claims, sexual harassment, and marketing practices. We share strategies, insights, and tales of woe.

Your tribe is your ticket to your best future. So let's figure out how to get you yours.

LITTLE CHANGES ACTION STEP: Name five tribes you belong to, or have belonged to, and do something to honor one of those tribes today.

60. ➡ Sam's Twenty Guidelines for Successful Tribe Building and Management

WHEN I SEE THE AMOUNT OF POSTURING, backbiting, stone-walling, power-mongering, and complaining that afflict many tribes, these points seem to need illumination. Some points apply more to business tribes (your clients, fan base, and peers), and others might work better for your family reunion, your choir group, your soccer club, or your knitting circle. Adapt at will.

1. The most important thing in any tribe is the vibe. (Some people might use the word *culture* instead of *vibe*, but my culture is such that I think it's more fun to say *vibe*.)

2. Pay attention to the people who understand you. You can probably afford to ignore the people who don't. For example, comedians only pay attention to the people who like and appreciate their jokes. They don't concern themselves with the people who think their act is rude, too loud, or inappropriate. Focus on the people who get you. Never try to convert, persuade, or bully anyone who's not already interested in what you're up to. Bless them and release them.

3. In seeming contradiction to guideline #2, remember that sometimes people in your tribe will argue with you or seem to pick on you. Assuming they're communicating via email, my policy is to wait one day, then write back thanking them for sharing their thoughts with me (hey, at least they care enough to be upset) and find as many things to agree with as I can, because usually there is some truth in what they're saying. I won't apologize for things I'm not sorry for, nor will I explain things that don't really concern them, but I will acknowledge that they have a good point and take appropriate action.

I can't count how many times, in both my public life and my private one, I've had someone write and criticize me for something I've said or done, and then, on receiving my response, immediately write back with great warmth, suddenly gentle as a lamb. Sometimes people just want to be heard.

And sometimes people will appear to reject you in order to get a special invitation. I call those the "come-in-and-get-me" emails. That's when someone writes me to say that as much as they'd like to, there's no way — not ever — that they could enroll in one of my workshops. So I wait a day, and then I write back and say that I completely understand. I add that if they should happen to change their mind, I would really love to welcome them into the group. Nine times out of ten, they enroll.

4. Express the truth of who you are in your communications with your tribe. If you have a dark sense of humor, use it. If you are sentimental and sappy, be that way. Don't worry about seeming too dark or sappy. Since your tribe is filled with like-minded people, they will love you for it. Suppressing your natural tendencies will flatten you out and make you boring — and you, my dear, are not boring. (Unless, of course, your tribal identity is "boring," in which case, go ahead and get some "Born to Be Mild" T-shirts made up.)

5. Explore nonverbal ways to express the truth of your tribe. Style, colors, rituals, pace, diet, habits, traditions, clothing, furnishings, greetings, and salutations can all help communicate and highlight the culture of your tribe.

6. If you click with people, stay in touch with them in a way that feels simple and fun. If you don't click with them, don't stay in touch. You want to stay in contact with the people who inspire you, who make you laugh, whom you trust. These are the people who summon up your best self and with whom you will do your best work. The people you don't trust, or who make you feel small, underappreciated, or misunderstood, are not worth your time. There's no need to be rude, of course. Just don't seek them out.

> You want to stay in contact with the people who inspire you, who make you laugh, whom you trust.

7. Only play tennis with better tennis players. Hang around people who are better at what you do than you are. Find the people you admire and respect and who treat you with respect. You might start out feeling outclassed, but eventually either you'll realize that you fit in all along or you'll raise your game.

8. It's good to belong to several tribes (cross-pollination can be wonderful), and it's good to not always be the one in charge. You may belong to a tribe of peers and lead a tribe of clients, fans, or staff.

9. Never say anything to anyone that you would not be happy to have attributed to you. Whether online or in person, if you would say it to the person's face, then fine. If not, keep it to yourself.

10. Be like the people you want to attract. So you want to attract people who pay their bills on time, show up when they say they will, and always give their best effort? Then make sure you are on point with your bill paying, punctuality, and effort. You want to attract friends who are cheerful, outgoing, and generous? Be that way, too.

11. Seek solutions that are not just win-win, but rather win-win-win-win-win. For example, when organizing my annual event, I look for opportunities and ways to structure the event that benefit the attendees, the speakers, the hotel, my team, and me. Last year, we gave each of the attendees a reusable water bottle as a registration gift. That made the attendees feel loved, and it also meant the speakers got a more alert audience, because everyone had an easy way to stay well hydrated. The hotel had less waste to deal with because we weren't leaving single-use water bottles behind, and it was a nice bit of marketing for my business that everyone went home with a treat that happened to have the Organized Artist Company's logo on it. Everybody won. Same thing goes for your charity gala, PTA meeting, or Zen archery collective — how can you create decisions, events, and policies that benefit everyone involved?

12. Be nice. Niceness is a highly underrated business and life skill. It's amazing how the impossible can become possible when you are calm and kindhearted with people. Have you ever seen people trying to yell or bully their way into a table at an overbooked restaurant? Did you notice that they are often not the people who get seated first? And they are almost never the people who get a free dessert.

13. Write out your partnership agreements, especially when money is involved. Take the time to clarify your agreements, expectations, and commitments. Be explicit about what you're willing to commit to and what the boundaries are. Don't assume that everyone is going to be just like you. Create a mutually acceptable exit strategy at the beginning, when everyone is still in a good mood. All partnerships end eventually, so you must decide from the outset how you would like that to happen.

> It's amazing how the impossible can become possible when you are calm and kindhearted with people.

14. Avoid barter. It makes me sad to say this, because, in principle, I love barter. In practice, though, I notice that everyone involved tends to feel like they're getting the losing part of the bargain. If you want to trade services with someone, I recommend that you simply write each other a check. For example, if Jeff is going to do Suzy's social media management in exchange for Suzy's taking care of Jeff's dogs three days a week, I would suggest that they decide on a fair price and each write the other a check for the same amount every month. This helps keep business as business, and if you're a freelancer, independent contractor, or small businessperson, charging market rates for your service makes you look and feel a lot more legitimate.

> Create a mutually acceptable exit strategy at the beginning, when everyone is still in a good mood.

15. Set boundaries for helping out the people in your tribe. It can be tough when your friend from tap-dance class starts asking you for your legal expertise, or when you get asked for your advice as a contractor during a cocktail party. My general rule is that if someone is asking me for something that will take me less than ten minutes to demonstrate, do, or explain, I'm happy to do it. Much more than that, though, and I gently direct their attention to my order form for private consultation. One exception: if the person asking the favor is a trusted peer, then I will usually help them without compensation, because it's in our mutual best interests to share.

16. Make sure that your tribe is giving you a good return on investment. Of course you want to contribute, but also make sure that you are nourished by the group and that the amount of time you spend on and with the tribe is commensurate with your reward. (Reward can be emotional, spiritual, intellectual, creative, financial, or some combination thereof.)

17. Don't rush relationships. Quality connections take time to build. Get to know people, stay low-key, and watch and learn from the group. The natural desire to be noticed and appreciated can give you that nervous seventh-grader feeling. Remembering that you are already loved (the Net) and that you have plenty of time to impress these people can give you the breathing room to make smart decisions.

18. As things begin, so they go. In my experience, when a project or relationship begins with missed communication, confusion, and weirdness, it almost never gets better. Keep a weather eye out for the flakes, nuts, and flimflam artists, and when you smell something sour, get out. (Be gracious, of course, but get out.) On the other hand, if things start out all groovy, flowing, fun, and easy, you may not need to wait for more evidence. Seal the deal.

When it comes to entering into deeper relationships with people in your tribe, trust your intuition. You are much better at sussing out other people than you give yourself credit for. You are very good at reading people when you allow yourself to know what you know. If you watch and listen carefully, you'll notice that people tell you exactly who they are within the first few minutes of knowing them.

19. Use your "values" words to communicate. If you're having trouble with a person or with a group, it can be great to remind them of your shared values. You might say, "The thing I've always loved about this group is how authentic and transparent we are with one another, and I really feel like we're falling off the mark on that." Or "You know, the thing I've always loved about you as a colleague is how inclusive you are, and honestly I've noticed you not being as inclusive lately, and I'm wondering if everything is okay." This also is good language to use to hold yourself accountable; saying something like "Look, I pride myself on being a good listener, and I feel like I have not been listening to you very well lately" can be an honorable way of acknowledging your shortcomings without getting into a lot of unnecessary self-punishment.

20. Enjoy frequent snacks. Food rituals are an important part of any tribe, and people are much more cheerful about showing up when they know there's going to be some good food. Good catering (even if that just means a nice cup of tea and a cookie) is a small expense when you consider how much loyalty and goodwill it generates.

LITTLE CHANGES ACTION STEP: Make a contribution to your tribe right now. This can be a social media post, a phone call, a financial donation, an act of service, or whatever you dream up.

61. ➡ Of Course You're Concerned about Not Fitting In

FOR THE EXTRA-SMART, the creative, the sensitive, or otherwise gifted person, building a tribe can be challenging partly because we are... weird. (I like to remember that the root meaning of *weird* has to do with destiny, from the Old English word *wyrd*, and it meant having the power to control destiny.) But we are weird because we are special. We were weird kids because we had talents and skills that were unusual or remarkable, and those talents and skills might have earned us some praise or attention from the grown-ups or our peers, or they might not have. I think we are afraid that if we give up our weirdness, we're giving up our specialness: that if we allow ourselves to be ordinary, we are giving up that which is extraordinary.

> We were the weird kids, the ones with a destiny, the ones who were not quite of this earth.

It's perfectly understandable that if you were the kid who stood along the far wall of the gym during the school dance, you might feel uneasy about putting yourself out there now. But trust me, there are people out there under the disco ball who will make you feel welcome.

So if this tribe talk is making you nervous, remember that you want to be around the *right* people. You want to be around the people who love you just as you are, who see you, and appreciate you, who help you, whom you can help. These people are not always hard to find, but it can take a bit of doing.

And maybe you're shy and introverted like me. (I know — no one ever believes it because I don't seem like the type, but I am quite the delicate flower.) And maybe you've had unfortunate experiences in groups before. It's time to get over it. We have to get over these perceived limitations because everything we want in life comes to us through other people. So we must get beyond our shyness. We must get beyond our fear. We have to get past our social history and find the other people that the Net is trying to connect us with, so that we can have what we say we want.

Many years ago, when I was working very hard to break myself of the habit of vicious self-loathing and self-criticism, I took myself out for a nice lunch at a little French bistro. This was unusual, because I wasn't used to treating myself as someone who could have a nice lunch by herself for no particular reason. Buoyed by the lunch, I decided to walk two blocks to a used bookstore that I liked. As I started to cross one of the side streets, a car was coming down the road at a speed that made it hard to tell whether it was going to stop to let me cross. At the last minute, the driver slowed down, and as I walked to the far sidewalk, I thought, "Yes, that's right — they should have stopped. I have the right of way. I have a right to be here."

Suddenly it felt like the world had slid sideways. I had never before had the thought, "I have a right to be here." Quite the contrary, I had spent my whole life acting like I did not have the right to be on the planet at all. I acted like I had to work as hard as I could in order to earn the right to be here. I constantly felt as though I didn't belong, as though I was slaving to keep my place. I had felt myself to be an alien. The thought that I belonged dazzled me: I felt dizzy and light-headed. I was so unnerved that I even staggered a bit and had to brace myself against the wall of the building I was passing as the thought echoed through my mind: I have a right to be here.

If you've never thought about it either, go ahead and say it out loud: I have a right to be here. I have a right to take up this much space. I have a right to think my thoughts and share my gifts and participate in this life.

I walked into the used bookstore, which was a ramshackle rabbit warren of a place with books stacked floor to ceiling, and found an out-of-the-way overstuffed armchair in a corner. I sat there for quite a while, imagining how different my life could be if I acted like I had the right to be present for it.

How much less apologizing would I do? How much less overwork? What if, on being invited to a party, I actually believed the hostess when she said, "No, don't bring anything — your presence is enough"? What if I believed it when people said, "Just be yourself"? What if I could just be me, here, sitting in this lumpy armchair, and that was sufficient?

Later, once the idea had had a chance to settle, I used it as a teaching story, and one of my students, an actor named Chris, still seeks me out on social media to tell me how much it has meant to him over the years to remember, whether he is out with friends or in the office of a casting director or onstage, that he has a right to be there.

> You are the perfect age and the perfect weight, and you have the perfect temperament to be you.

You are needed and necessary to this planet right now, exactly as you are this minute. You are the perfect age and the perfect weight, and you have the perfect temperament to be you. No one else can do it. We need you. You not only have the right to be here on this earth in this moment, but you have the privilege. Enjoy it while it lasts.

LITTLE CHANGES ACTION STEP: Claim your right to be exactly here — wherever you are — in whatever way you like.

62. ➡ Be the Elusive Rainbow Sparkles Unicorn

IT'S NOT WRONG TO FEEL a sense of dread when you know you have to confront a big room filled with people. Even for the most sociable of creatures, figuring out what to say, what to wear, and how to act in any new setting, from conferences to cocktail parties, can be daunting. And for those of us who have a touch of social anxiety, are introverted, shy, or simply hate crowds, it's easy to just want to stay home in bed with a nice, long historical novel and a bowl of popcorn. (I know there are those who adore being in groups and who don't care to have a lot of time alone, and while this mystifies me, I so admire you.)

Everything good in your life has come to you through other people. And it's hard to meet new people when you're hiding in bed — or, as is more common these days, behind your computer. Getting out and meeting new colleagues, clients, and friends is beneficial to your life, your spirit, and your work.

So, just in time, here is my idiosyncratic guide to having a fun and profitable time in a group.

Step 1. Be the elusive rainbow sparkles unicorn. You are not one of the crowd; you are special. Your time is precious, and your energy reserves are limited. You are not there to meet every single person or to hand out every single one of your business cards.

Start thinking of yourself as a bit of a celebrity. You don't need to be at every event — in fact, it's better if you aren't. Show up to the events that interest you, look fabulous (see step 6), and don't be afraid of being a bit mysterious.

Step 2. Achieve a minigoal, then take a break. Think of one small win that would make the day, the evening, or the event worthwhile, and once it's done, give yourself permission to slack off a bit.

Maybe there's one person with whom you'd particularly like to connect, or, at a conference, one topic you'd like to learn more about. Setting a minigoal for any given session gives you an "object of the game" for each block of time. For example, you may decide that during the keynote you want to get at least three ideas you can turn into blog posts. During lunch you might want to sit next to someone you don't know, ask them open-ended questions, and just listen as they tell you about themselves (see step 5).

This strategy gives you a valuable end point, so if you start to feel tired, pressured, or overwhelmed, you can check to see if you've achieved your minigoal and if you have, take a break. It's amazing what a quick fifteen minutes in a quiet room can do for a person.

I'm not much of a yogi, but when I need to refuel, I often assume this restorative pose: I lie on the floor with my legs up on the bed, or up the wall. Something about having your feet higher than your head while your spine is flat on the floor is both restful and calmly invigorating.

Other energizing options include taking a catnap, going for a walk outside, washing your face and hands, or doing a little light reading. Don't try to do work or check email — that will just stress you out. Give yourself whatever you need to stay cheerful over the long haul.

Step 3. Set an audacious goal. I once attended a smallish convention having decided that I wanted the trip to generate at least ten thousand dollars for my business. I didn't worry about the

how, I just set the audacious goal and kept my eyes open for opportunities. Sure enough, by the time I got on the plane home, I
had entered into a joint venture that ended up grossing well over
my goal.

Your audacious goal may be to uncover the brilliant idea that
will enable you to double your sales. Maybe you'd like to find a
like-minded parent in your community, find a way to get nation-
wide press, or come across a new project idea that will transform
your home. Don't concern yourself with whether you think your
audacious goal is realistic or not. You don't need to know exactly
how you might achieve this goal — that is part of the mystery,
part of the invitation, and part of the adventure.

You may decide to keep your audacious goal to yourself and
think of it as a secret mission, or you may find yourself wanting to
share it. It's remarkable how swiftly dreams can come true when
you open up to smart, supportive people.

Step 4. Let Destiny have her way with you. Just for fun, assume that anyone near you has been placed there for a reason. You
may just quietly observe them, or you may want to reach out and
introduce yourself. Either way, stay present, notice details, and
don't make routine assumptions. What news, lesson, or message
does this person have for you right now?

Step 5. Listen. Whenever I go to a party, I remind myself that
my only job as a good guest is to listen. I make it a practice to
give my undivided attention to whoever is in front of me (no
Hollywood-style scanning of the room to see if there's someone
more interesting around), and as I listen, I try to maintain gentle
eye contact and hold the thought that this person is entirely wonderful, exactly as they are.

Not only does this strategy free me up from having to think
of clever things to say, it also gives me a reputation as a very nice
person. In fact, active listening is so powerful that you may be

surprised by how strongly other people respond to you. They may get slightly giddy from the attention you're paying them, and they may start sharing confidences. Some people become so unnerved that they will actually walk away from you rather abruptly. That's okay. Keep your own boundaries firmly in place, and don't take anything personally.

It's amazing how easy it is to relax when you concentrate solely on making someone else feel welcomed, seen, and heard.

Step 6. Look great. When you feel like you look good, there's an extra bounce in your step and an extra twinkle in your eye, so it's worth investing time and money in your appearance.

I'm not saying you have to be dressed in the height of fashion or spend a fortune on new things, but make sure your clothes are clean and in good repair. Nothing is more unflattering (not to mention uncomfortable) than clothes that don't fit, so be blazingly honest with yourself and, if necessary, go up or down a size or two to arrive at a look that's just right. This is no time for "sizing vanity." Manufacturers' sizes are all over the map, and while a medium size might work from one designer, another brand may require you to buy the large. The size you wear is not a judgment on your fabulousness, your attractiveness, or your worth — it's just a number on the tag that I highly recommend you cut out and forget.

You might want to consider getting a new hairstyle (yes, even the men). If you wear makeup, having an event to go to is a great excuse to get a makeover at a specialty store or one of the department store makeup counters. A fresh look can make you feel years younger, and there are some wonderful new products, formulations, and cosmetic tricks that can truly work wonders.

A special word about shoes: my extremely sophisticated grandmother often said that you could always tell a lady by her shoes. As in most things, she was right, and this rule goes double for gentlemen. Good shoes convey professionalism, good taste, and self-respect. Whether you are going to be swirling around the ballroom or tromping around the convention center, your feet deserve the best. Never cheap out on shoes.

Remember, too, that there's likely to be a bunch of photos taken of you at these events — selfies, group shots, and new memories in the making — and you'll have a brighter smile in all of them if you know you look terrific.

Step 7. Create your follow-up plan in advance. The fortune, they say, is in the follow-up. So block out some time the day after an event to write thank-you notes, make phone calls, and schedule appointments with all the people who said they were interested in what you do. (Not all of them actually *are* interested, of course — some of them were just being polite — but you'll never know if you don't ask.)

> Never cheap out on shoes.

Think of a fun, sincere, personalized way to stay in touch with the one or two or twenty or two thousand people who got to meet you, hear you speak, or otherwise engage with you. There's no sense getting all duded up to go to a party or event, turning on the charm, and then coming home with a stack of business cards that you then ignore.

LITTLE CHANGES ACTION STEP: What event is next on your calendar? Write down one goal or result you would like to see come of that event and one follow-up step that you could joyfully do.

63. ➤ Are You in the Right Tribe?

WORKING QUICKLY and without thinking too much, write down the answers to these questions:

1. If you could imagine a world that is just like this one but slightly better, in what way would it be better?
2. What is a quality of your mother (or favorite mother figure) that you love and admire?
3. What is a quality of your father (or favorite father figure) that you love and admire?
4. What is a quality of one of your close friends that you love and admire?
5. What is a quality that you have been praised for (whether you agree with it or not)?

These words reflect your own best qualities (surprise!) and the qualities that are also characteristic of the people you most enjoy being around. They reflect your values. Have a checklist of these words, and look for people who match.

LITTLE CHANGES ACTION STEP: Look at the people in the groups you're involved with now. Do they match these values? If not, then don't waste your time on them, no matter how good they look on paper.

64. ➤ There I Am

CHOOSING TO BELIEVE THE BEST about people is an important part of my spiritual discipline. I work hard to refrain from judging other people, even when they are making it very, very hard to not judge them. I have come to realize that judgment is not really my job. The more I seek out the good in each person, the more good I find. I don't mind if others find this attitude Pollyannaish. I am not blind to the shallow, cruel, thoughtless, selfish, and just plain mean actions of others — I simply choose to look past them.

> I work hard to refrain from judging other people, even when they are making it very, very hard to not judge them.

I find it relaxing to concentrate on how alike we all are, and how much we are like our ancestors. I enjoy imagining families thousands of years ago in faraway lands having dinner together: the uncle who tells bawdy jokes, the teenager who feels misunderstood, the glimmer in the eye of the young woman who's just fallen in love for the second time. Can't you picture them now? I find our homogeneity endearing.

Focusing on our sameness has also helped me get past an unfortunate tendency to want to criticize others. I'm a pretty tolerant person, but occasionally I find myself thinking, "Nope. You are just not allowed to be like that." I get grouchy around people who have a daddy's-little-princess attitude, and I deplore willful ignorance. Teasing gets my hackles up, especially when grown-ups tease children, and I get annoyed whenever people appear cynical and bored by the world. So now, whenever I see someone of whom I disapprove, I think: "There I am."

A group of rowdy boys being obnoxious: there I am. Someone who is life-threateningly overweight: there I am. An extremely beautiful, elegantly dressed person: there I am. An exasperated mother at the supermarket: there I am. Her whining child: there I am.

I think it's funny that we feel like other people are different from us, because clearly we're exactly the same. If you took all of humanity, stripped us naked, put us on the universe's biggest football field, took two steps back, and squinted a bit, you wouldn't be able to tell us apart. You would not be able to see any difference between the shortest person and the tallest person. You would not be able to tell the difference between men and women. You would not be able to detect the very slight degrees of change in skin tone, weight, or age that we see as so dramatic. Basically, we're identical. When I remember that, it's easier for me to look at someone with whom I disagree and remember how much we have in common.

> If you took all of humanity, stripped us naked, put us on the universe's biggest football field, took two steps back, and squinted a bit, you wouldn't be able to tell us apart.

We all want the same things. Everybody wants to be loved and appreciated. Everybody wants to feel like their work matters. Everybody wants to raise beautiful children and eat food and laugh and tell good stories and get a good night's sleep. When I remember that, it's easier for me to feel compassion for the people who upset me.

So here we all are. We look exactly alike, we want exactly the same things, and we communicate in very much the same ways. Most human communication is nonverbal, and many of our gestures and postures transcend both time and culture. People have always covered their mouths when laughing. People have always tightened up when being reprimanded. People have always glowered when they're angry and cooed and clucked to entertain babies. We share the same physical language. (Desmond Morris's 1977 book *Manwatching* is, I believe, out of print and a bit dated, but still makes for fascinating reading with wonderful, evocative photographs.) When I watch people blush, scowl, grin, cry, or hug in the way that people always have, it's easier for me to remember that we are all one family.

We do insist, however, on making a big deal about the minor differences that remain. He's a Democrat. She's French. He's a vegan. She's rich. Black. White. Pacific Islander. New Yorker. Queer. Decaf mocha latte with no foam. Like it matters. I remember reading somewhere once that if aliens came to Earth, they would be surprised not by how violent we are, but how peaceable. It's unusual that mammals as large as we are can live — indeed, seek to live — at such close quarters. Chimpanzees need almost one hundred square yards for their "natural home range" and spend their days in subgroups with just eight to ten adults.* But we humans love to crowd ourselves into dining rooms, shopping malls, apartment buildings, and stadiums. When I think that most of the time we humans interact calmly, even in large groups, it is easier for me to see acts of violence and destruction as anomalies rather than evidence of our baseness.

I know, too, that personal identity is not nearly as fixed as we like to tell ourselves it is. Being adaptable is one of our best survival mechanisms. We adjust almost immediately to things that, before we do them, seem impossible. Even the most extreme

---

* Jordi Casamitjana, "Enclosure Size in Captive Wild Mammals: A Comparison between UK Zoological Collections and the Wild," Captive Animals' Protection Society, www.captiveanimals.org/wp-content/uploads/2011/02 /Enclosure-size.pdf, accessed June 15, 2016).

situations can become the "new normal" in a shockingly short time. Disaster workers adapt to horrible sights and smells, prisoners adjust to the rules and hierarchies of jail time, and if you're among the nearly 80 percent of adults who become parents, you know how quickly a person can get used to the life-upending effect of a new baby in the house. Heck, I bet some of you have even gotten used to the horrors of sitting in an office chair all day. You may say that you hate change, but change sure loves you. When I remember how swiftly we can change our behavior based on circumstance, it's easier for me to understand how crowds can get disorderly, how bureaucrats can forget how to laugh, and how peer pressure can trigger cruel words and inconsiderate actions.

> You may say that you hate change, but change sure loves you.

So I see all of these similarities in people, and yet I also notice that you, my dear, are completely one of a kind, and your special combination of qualities is baked in. No one sees the world quite the way you do, and no one processes information in quite the same way you do. And once you are gone, your particular brand of you-ness will never come again. This is why it is so important for you to do the work that only you can do while you are still here to do it. When I remember that your body and your personality are irreproducible and that your time here is fleeting, it is easy for me to cherish you. I see your uniqueness, and I think, "There I am."

The minute I think, "There I am," I feel myself melt. I am jolted out of my superiority complex and into the memory of our oneness. I see my sisters and brothers, and how frail and flawed we all are. I feel the Net. I see my mirror.

LITTLE CHANGES ACTION STEP: Think of a person of whom you disapprove and list five ways in which you two are exactly the same. Let the divinity within you acknowledge the divinity within them. Namaste.

65. ➡ You Can't Take Everyone with You

YOU MAY HAVE HEARD THE QUOTE from the businessperson and motivational speaker Jim Rohn: "You are the average of the five people you spend the most time with." In other words, if you look at the five people you hang out with the most, you are probably right in the middle of the pack in terms of weight, income, productivity, positivity, and prestige.

So, as you change your life, you will almost inevitably find yourself changing your cast of companions. You may also have the urge to try to get your current group to change along with you. I can pretty much guarantee you that only one of these strategies will work.

In fact, my friend Shasta Nelson, the author of *Friendships Don't Just Happen*, writes that we lose half our close friends every seven years and replace them with new relationships. This usually happens gradually, and the change in our social or work groups feels perfectly natural and undramatic. My clients often get nervous that they're going to have to break up with their friends or family as their lives or fortunes change, but that's not usually the case. As you get deeper into the world of entrepreneurship, or spiritual development, or disc golf, or manga, or whatever is calling to you, you automatically make time in your schedule and in your heart for that new community. As anyone who's ever had a second child will tell you, the additional community does not take love away from the first: rather it enhances and deepens your love for all of your communities.

New converts often want to spread the gospel to all their old friends. "This would be so great for so-and-so!" you think. "I can't wait to bring them with me to the next event!" Rookie mistake. While it's possible that one or two people from your former life will want to do what you're doing, it's highly unlikely. Which is entirely fine. Understand that their lack of enthusiasm is not a commentary on you. And even though you are on fire for your newfound interest, you may want to do everyone a favor and find some other, more mutually agreeable topics for conversation.

> While it's possible that one or two people from your former life will want to do what you're doing, it's highly unlikely. Which is entirely fine.

Everyone has their own road. Be as respectful of their path as you would like them to be of yours. Not everyone is interested in your road. You cannot take everyone along with you, but that's not a reason to stay put. *Not* moving because you're afraid you're going to leave someone behind isn't going to work for either of you. Be kind, be clear, and keep walking.

Finally, just because a relationship ends doesn't mean it failed. So it is possible that what feels like a death and a loss and a sacrifice is actually an invitation to a much, much, much better life.

LITTLE CHANGES ACTION STEP: Take a moment to reflect on some of the people who have cycled through your life. Some have come and gone and then come back again, others have moved on permanently. Make a 5-Minute Art greeting card (that you never have to send) for one person who comes to mind as you think of this.

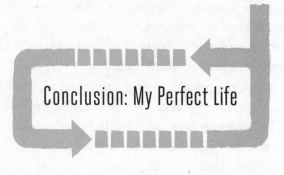

Conclusion: My Perfect Life

TODAY WAS AN AMAZING DAY. I woke up just before dawn, and I watched the Santa Ynez mountains and the sky turn from dark blue to pink to full, warm daylight while I had my morning tea and did my daily prayer/meditation work. I had a terrific consultation with a client in the United Kingdom who's growing her business by leaps and bounds. I taught a good class online, and I cleaned up some administrative stuff that had been hanging about. I did a bit of writing. I took a nap. I had one of those deliciously long, chatty, talk-about-everything-and-nothing conversations with my sister. Luke and I took our beach walk, and then I cooked dinner. (I make a heck of a nice roast chicken. The trick is to rub it with butter and sea salt, maybe put some thinly sliced garlic under the skin, put it on a roasting rack with a half-cup of water in the bottom of the pan to prevent scorching, then cook it at a very high heat — 450°F — in a pan on a roasting rack for about fifteen minutes per pound without disturbing it: no basting required. Magic.)

Sometimes you hear songs or stories about not noticing the good times until they're gone. About realizing that the ordinary moments were the most precious ones. I like to think that the mindfulness practices I use and have put in this book have enabled me to appreciate my life as it unfolds. I experience gratitude in each present moment, rather than in retrospect.

Your extraordinary future is now. You are worth it. You have talents and skills that the world needs now. There is no later moment in which the fullness of your expression will be more appropriate, more necessary, or more desirable. Your mistakes are perfect. Your journey up to now has been perfect. And you are perfectly positioned to become your slightly future self.

As you model self-honoring behavior, you may teach others. Or not. As you allow your talents to shine, you may inspire others. Or not. As you refuse to belittle yourself or others, you may encourage a more loving environment for all. Or not. You are responsible to yourself. Let the world spin as it will.

We know we are only here for a short time, but we don't act like we know that. You will not have unlimited opportunities to do your work, so do it now. There will come a time when you can no longer express your love, so express it now. There will come a time when all of your possessions are just stuff, and when all of your plans and excuses are just air. Your moment is now.

When we are completely engaged in the present moment, it enraptures us. There is a beauty to its presence and its passing. We feel kissed by time, rather than punished by it.

My wish for you is in that kiss.

Acknowledgments

THIS BOOK WAS INSPIRED and fueled by the work of every teacher I've ever had and every book I've ever read, and I'm so indebted to the following friends, writers, mentors, family members, and tribal leaders for their insight, wisdom, humor, creativity, and deep love. The smart stuff is all theirs; the errors are all mine.

An extra-special thanks to this book's fairy godmother, the ingenious Carol Allen.

Alexandra Goetz
Amanda Swann
Amy Ahlers
Amy Jo Goddard
Andrea Goetz
Angelique Rewers
Anne McQuary
Augusten Burroughs
Bari Baumgardner
Beatrice Briggs
Ben Saltzman
Bill Baren
Byron Katie

Cheryl Strayed
Christine Arylo
Colleen Gallion
Constance Kent
Daga Ramsey
Dave Razowsky
David Neagle
Ed O'Neill
Elizabeth Manning
Erika Büky
Foster Goetz
Gay Hendricks
Georgia Hughes

Gunnar Bennett

James Hallett

Jennifer Hardaway

Jennifer Lee

Jen Raim

Kay Banks

Kim Corbin

Kristen Cashman

Laura Bennett

Leonore Tjia

Linda Sivertson

Luke Hannington

Lynn Martin

Maggie Ostara

Margaret Weber

Martin de Maat

Maryann Udel

Melissa McFarlane

Michael Gellman

Michael Gerber

Rev. Michael Kosik

Monique Muhlenkamp

Munro Magruder

Peter Walsh

Phil Dyer

Philip Goetz

Phil Swann

Rhonda Britten

Ron West

Sam Christensen

SARK (Susan Ariel Rainbow
   Kennedy)

Seth Godin

Shasta Nelson

Stephanie Miller

Stephanie Tuss

Stephen Mitchell

Stephen Ramsey

Tiffany Cruise-Johnson

Tish Hicks

Tom Casey

Tracy Brown

Virginia Briggs

Rev. Dr. William Thomas, Jr.

Index

About the Author

ORIGINALLY FROM CHICAGO, Sam Bennett is a writer, speaker, actor, teacher, creativity/productivity specialist, and the author of the bestselling *Get It Done: From Procrastination to Creative Genius in 15 Minutes a Day* (New World Library). She is the creator of www.TheOrganizedArtistCompany.com, dedicated to helping creative people get unstuck, especially by helping them focus and move forward on their goals. Now based in a tiny beach town outside Los Angeles, Bennett offers workshops, keynotes, and private consulting. She also makes a heck of a roast chicken.